*Start Your Own*

# GREEN BUSINESS

D1119659

Additional titles in *Entrepreneur's **Startup Series***

## *Start Your Own*

*Arts and Crafts Business*

*Bar and Club*

*Bed & Breakfast*

*Business on eBay*

*Business Support Service*

*Car Wash*

*Child Care Service*

*Cleaning Service*

*Clothing Store*

*Coin-Operated Laundry*

*Consulting*

*e-Business*

*e-Learning Business*

*Event Planning Business*

*Executive Recruiting Service*

*Freight Brokerage Business*

*Gift Basket Service*

*Grant-Writing Business*

*Home Inspection Service*

*Import/Export Business*

*Information Consultant Business*

*Law Practice*

*Lawn Care Business*

*Mail Order Business*

*Medical Claims Billing Service*

*Personal Concierge Service*

*Personal Training Business*

*Pet-Sitting Business*

*Restaurant and Five Other Food Businesses*

*Self-Publishing Business*

*Seminar Production Business*

*Specialty Travel & Tour Business*

*Staffing Service*

*Successful Retail Business*

*Vending Business*

*Wedding Consultant Business*

*Wholesale Distribution Business*

Entrepreneur
MAGAZINE'S

# start*up*

## Start Your Own

# GREEN
# BUSINESS

*Your Step-by-Step*
*Guide to Success*

*Entrepreneur Press and Rich Mintzer*

EP
Entrepreneur
Press

Jere L. Calmes, Publisher
Managing Editor: Marla Markman
Cover Design: Beth Hansen-Winter
Production and Composition: Eliot House Productions

© 2009 by Entrepreneur Media Inc.
All rights reserved.

Reproduction or translation of any part of this work beyond that permitted by Section 107 or 108 of the 1976 United States Copyright Act without permission of the copyright owner is unlawful. Requests for permission or further information should be addressed to the Business Products Division, Entrepreneur Media Inc.

This publication is designed to provide accurate and authoritative information in regard to the subject matter covered. It is sold with the understanding that the publisher is not engaged in rendering legal, accounting or other professional services. If legal advice or other expert assistance is required, the services of a competent professional person should be sought.

**Library of Congress Cataloging-in-Publication Data available**

ISBN-13: 978-1-59918-339-8
ISBN-10: 1-59918-339-0

Printed in Canada

13 12 11 10 09                                          10 9 8 7 6 5 4 3 2 1

# Contents

Acknowledgments . . . . . . . . . . . . . . . . . . . . . . . . . . . . xi
Preface . . . . . . . . . . . . . . . . . . . . . . . . . . . . . . . . . xiii

*Chapter 1*
## What Does "Green" Mean? . . . . . . . . . . . . . . . . . . . . . 1
Looking Forward and Looking Back . . . . . . . . . . . . . 2
Sustainability . . . . . . . . . . . . . . . . . . . . . . . . . . . . . 3
The Eco-Lifecycle of a Product . . . . . . . . . . . . . . . . 6
The Green Mindset . . . . . . . . . . . . . . . . . . . . . . . . 7
What Does a Green Office Look Like? . . . . . . . . . . . 9
Have You Ever Stepped Into a Green Store? . . . . . . . 10
Have You Been to a Green Factory Lately? . . . . . . . . 10
The Green Homebased Businesses . . .
   Have You Seen One? . . . . . . . . . . . . . . . . . . . . . . 11
Balancing Pragmatic Business Concerns
   with an Environmental Approach . . . . . . . . . . . . . 11

*Chapter 2*
## Business Decisions . . . . . . . . . . . . . . . . . . . . . . . . . 15
What Are Your Personal Goals? . . . . . . . . . . . . . . . . 16
What Are Your Financial Goals? . . . . . . . . . . . . . . . 18

What Are Your Business Goals? . . . . . . . . . . . . . . . . . . . . . . . . . 18
What Are Your Environmental Goals? . . . . . . . . . . . . . . . . . . . . . 20
How to Choose the Right Business . . . . . . . . . . . . . . . . . . . . . . 22
    Are You Inclined to Sell? . . . . . . . . . . . . . . . . . . . . . . . . . . . 22
    Can You Provide a Service? . . . . . . . . . . . . . . . . . . . . . . . . . 23
    Into Manufacturing? . . . . . . . . . . . . . . . . . . . . . . . . . . . . . . 24
Suit Yourself . . . . . . . . . . . . . . . . . . . . . . . . . . . . . . . . . . . . . 25
There's No Need to Re-Invent the Wheel:
    A Look at 22 Successful Green Businesses . . . . . . . . . . . . . . 26
    1. Pangea Organics . . . . . . . . . . . . . . . . . . . . . . . . . . . . . . . 26
    2. Patagonia . . . . . . . . . . . . . . . . . . . . . . . . . . . . . . . . . . . . 27
    3. New Belgium Brewery . . . . . . . . . . . . . . . . . . . . . . . . . . 27
    4. Clif Bar & Company . . . . . . . . . . . . . . . . . . . . . . . . . . . . 27
    5. Green Mountain Coffee Roasters . . . . . . . . . . . . . . . . . . 28
    6. Kettle Foods . . . . . . . . . . . . . . . . . . . . . . . . . . . . . . . . . . 28
    7. Seventh Generation . . . . . . . . . . . . . . . . . . . . . . . . . . . . 29
    8. Pizza Fusion . . . . . . . . . . . . . . . . . . . . . . . . . . . . . . . . . . 29
    9. The Evergreen Group LLC and Green Key Real Estate . . 30
    10. Solar Wind Works . . . . . . . . . . . . . . . . . . . . . . . . . . . . . 30
    11. WeWe Clothing . . . . . . . . . . . . . . . . . . . . . . . . . . . . . . . 31
    12. Newman's Own Organics . . . . . . . . . . . . . . . . . . . . . . . 31
    13. Odorzout . . . . . . . . . . . . . . . . . . . . . . . . . . . . . . . . . . . 32
    14. Inu Treats . . . . . . . . . . . . . . . . . . . . . . . . . . . . . . . . . . . 32
    15. GreeNow . . . . . . . . . . . . . . . . . . . . . . . . . . . . . . . . . . . . 33
    16. Chokola'j® . . . . . . . . . . . . . . . . . . . . . . . . . . . . . . . . . . . 33
    17. Selfish Box . . . . . . . . . . . . . . . . . . . . . . . . . . . . . . . . . . 34
    18. Sum-Bo-Shine . . . . . . . . . . . . . . . . . . . . . . . . . . . . . . . . 34
    19. Electric Body . . . . . . . . . . . . . . . . . . . . . . . . . . . . . . . . 35
    20. Montana Stones . . . . . . . . . . . . . . . . . . . . . . . . . . . . . . 35
    21. iTySE . . . . . . . . . . . . . . . . . . . . . . . . . . . . . . . . . . . . . . 36
    22. Wild Dill . . . . . . . . . . . . . . . . . . . . . . . . . . . . . . . . . . . . 36

Chapter 3
Customers and Market Research . . . . . . . . . . . . . . . . . . . . . . 39
    What Do Customers Want? . . . . . . . . . . . . . . . . . . . . . . . . . 40
    Exploring Your Target Market . . . . . . . . . . . . . . . . . . . . . . . 42
    Focus Groups . . . . . . . . . . . . . . . . . . . . . . . . . . . . . . . . . . . 44
    Utilizing Your Research . . . . . . . . . . . . . . . . . . . . . . . . . . . . 45
    Niche Markets . . . . . . . . . . . . . . . . . . . . . . . . . . . . . . . . . . . 46

Scouting the Competition . . . . . . . . . . . . . . . . . . . . . . . . . . . . . . . 47
The 80–20 Rule . . . . . . . . . . . . . . . . . . . . . . . . . . . . . . . . . . . . . . . 49
Common Market Research Errors . . . . . . . . . . . . . . . . . . . . . . . . 50

*Chapter 4*
**Building Your Green Business: Names,**
**Structures, Locations, and Energy Options . . . . . . . . . . . . . . 51**
Making Your Business Name Official . . . . . . . . . . . . . . . . . . . . . 53
Business Structures . . . . . . . . . . . . . . . . . . . . . . . . . . . . . . . . . . . 54
Zoning Regulations . . . . . . . . . . . . . . . . . . . . . . . . . . . . . . . . . . . 57
Finding a Green Location . . . . . . . . . . . . . . . . . . . . . . . . . . . . . . 58
Know Your Business Needs . . . . . . . . . . . . . . . . . . . . . . . . . . . . . 60
Building Green from the Ground Up . . . . . . . . . . . . . . . . . . . . . 61
Leasing Versus Buying and Building . . . . . . . . . . . . . . . . . . . . . 62
Finding a Green Builder, Architect, and/or Contractor . . . . . . . 63
Brownfields . . . . . . . . . . . . . . . . . . . . . . . . . . . . . . . . . . . . . . . . . 64
Energy Options . . . . . . . . . . . . . . . . . . . . . . . . . . . . . . . . . . . . . . 65
Solar Panels and Wind Turbines . . . . . . . . . . . . . . . . . . . . . . . . 66

*Chapter 5*
**Business Equipment, Furniture,**
**and Figuring Out Your Costs . . . . . . . . . . . . . . . . . . . . . . . . . . 69**
Startup Costs . . . . . . . . . . . . . . . . . . . . . . . . . . . . . . . . . . . . . . . . 70
Computer Considerations . . . . . . . . . . . . . . . . . . . . . . . . . . . . . . 70
Printers and Eco-Friendly Ways of Using Them . . . . . . . . . . . . 73
Telephone Systems . . . . . . . . . . . . . . . . . . . . . . . . . . . . . . . . . . . 74
Other Equipment . . . . . . . . . . . . . . . . . . . . . . . . . . . . . . . . . . . . 74
Greener Office Supplies . . . . . . . . . . . . . . . . . . . . . . . . . . . . . . . 75
Green Office Furniture . . . . . . . . . . . . . . . . . . . . . . . . . . . . . . . . 76
    Chairs and Lighting . . . . . . . . . . . . . . . . . . . . . . . . . . . . . . . . 78
Green Printing . . . . . . . . . . . . . . . . . . . . . . . . . . . . . . . . . . . . . . 79
Website Designers . . . . . . . . . . . . . . . . . . . . . . . . . . . . . . . . . . . 80
Startup Costs Revisited . . . . . . . . . . . . . . . . . . . . . . . . . . . . . . . 81
Operating Costs . . . . . . . . . . . . . . . . . . . . . . . . . . . . . . . . . . . . . 84

*Chapter 6*
**Getting the Green to Go Green . . . . . . . . . . . . . . . . . . . . . . . . 87**
Green Financing . . . . . . . . . . . . . . . . . . . . . . . . . . . . . . . . . . . . . 88
Finding Funding . . . . . . . . . . . . . . . . . . . . . . . . . . . . . . . . . . . . . 89

The All-Important Business Plan . . . . . . . . . . . . . . . . . . . . . . . . . 90
   Components of a Business Plan . . . . . . . . . . . . . . . . . . . . . . 91
   Reviewing Your Business Plan . . . . . . . . . . . . . . . . . . . . . . 94
Your Sustainability Plan . . . . . . . . . . . . . . . . . . . . . . . . . . . . . . 96
Your Waste Management Plan . . . . . . . . . . . . . . . . . . . . . . . . . . 96
Personal Loans . . . . . . . . . . . . . . . . . . . . . . . . . . . . . . . . . . . . . 97
Government Financing . . . . . . . . . . . . . . . . . . . . . . . . . . . . . . . 98
Other Options . . . . . . . . . . . . . . . . . . . . . . . . . . . . . . . . . . . . . . 99
Financing on Your Own . . . . . . . . . . . . . . . . . . . . . . . . . . . . . 100

**Chapter 7**

**Making Your Way in a Greener World** . . . . . . . . . . . . . . . . . . 101
Making Money . . . . . . . . . . . . . . . . . . . . . . . . . . . . . . . . . . . . 102
Knowledge . . . . . . . . . . . . . . . . . . . . . . . . . . . . . . . . . . . . . . . 102
Pricing . . . . . . . . . . . . . . . . . . . . . . . . . . . . . . . . . . . . . . . . . . 103
Inventory . . . . . . . . . . . . . . . . . . . . . . . . . . . . . . . . . . . . . . . . 105
Ordering from Green Suppliers . . . . . . . . . . . . . . . . . . . . . . . 106
Manufacturing Environmentally-Friendly Products . . . . . . . . . 107
Growing It Yourself . . . . . . . . . . . . . . . . . . . . . . . . . . . . . . . . 108
Sustainable Packaging and Packing . . . . . . . . . . . . . . . . . . . . 109
Greener Shipping . . . . . . . . . . . . . . . . . . . . . . . . . . . . . . . . . . 111
Greener Service with a Smile . . . . . . . . . . . . . . . . . . . . . . . . . 111
Greener Commuting . . . . . . . . . . . . . . . . . . . . . . . . . . . . . . . 112
Teaming with Likeminded Companies . . . . . . . . . . . . . . . . . . 113

**Chapter 8**

**People Power: Your Green Team and Your Community** . . . 115
Establishing a Green Business Culture . . . . . . . . . . . . . . . . . . 117
A Green Team . . . . . . . . . . . . . . . . . . . . . . . . . . . . . . . . . . . . 119
Green Protocol . . . . . . . . . . . . . . . . . . . . . . . . . . . . . . . . . . . 120
Building a Collective (or "Team") Mindset . . . . . . . . . . . . . . . 121
Your Community . . . . . . . . . . . . . . . . . . . . . . . . . . . . . . . . . . 122
The Homebased Business . . . . . . . . . . . . . . . . . . . . . . . . . . . . 124

**Chapter 9**

**Spreading the Word: Marketing,
Promotion, and Advertising** . . . . . . . . . . . . . . . . . . . . . . . . 127
Marketing Stories: The Good . . . . . . . . . . . . . . . . . . . . . . . . . 128

And the Bad . . . . . . . . . . . . . . . . . . . . . . . . . . . . . . . . . . . . . . 130
Green Marketing . . . . . . . . . . . . . . . . . . . . . . . . . . . . . . . . . . 130
Having a Plan . . . . . . . . . . . . . . . . . . . . . . . . . . . . . . . . . . . . 132
Promoting Products and Services . . . . . . . . . . . . . . . . . . . . . 133
Public Relations . . . . . . . . . . . . . . . . . . . . . . . . . . . . . . . . . . 135
Press Releases 101 . . . . . . . . . . . . . . . . . . . . . . . . . . . . . . . . 137
Your Company Website . . . . . . . . . . . . . . . . . . . . . . . . . . . . . 141
Online Newsletters . . . . . . . . . . . . . . . . . . . . . . . . . . . . . . . . 142
Blogging . . . . . . . . . . . . . . . . . . . . . . . . . . . . . . . . . . . . . . . . 144
Advertising 101 . . . . . . . . . . . . . . . . . . . . . . . . . . . . . . . . . . 144
    Fliers, Brochures, and More . . . . . . . . . . . . . . . . . . . . . . . 145
    Newspapers and Magazines . . . . . . . . . . . . . . . . . . . . . . . 145
    The Internet . . . . . . . . . . . . . . . . . . . . . . . . . . . . . . . . . . 146
    Radio . . . . . . . . . . . . . . . . . . . . . . . . . . . . . . . . . . . . . . . 146
    Television . . . . . . . . . . . . . . . . . . . . . . . . . . . . . . . . . . . . 147
    Headlines . . . . . . . . . . . . . . . . . . . . . . . . . . . . . . . . . . . . 148

*Chapter 10*
**Social Responsibility** . . . . . . . . . . . . . . . . . . . . . . . . . . . . . **157**
It Starts at Home . . . . . . . . . . . . . . . . . . . . . . . . . . . . . . . . . 158
Doing for Others . . . . . . . . . . . . . . . . . . . . . . . . . . . . . . . . . 159
Fair Trade Practices . . . . . . . . . . . . . . . . . . . . . . . . . . . . . . . 160
A Green Work Environment . . . . . . . . . . . . . . . . . . . . . . . . . 161
Green Education . . . . . . . . . . . . . . . . . . . . . . . . . . . . . . . . . . 163
Giving Your People What They Want . . . . . . . . . . . . . . . . . . 164
Socially Responsible Investing . . . . . . . . . . . . . . . . . . . . . . . . 165

*Chapter 11*
**Keeping It Going** . . . . . . . . . . . . . . . . . . . . . . . . . . . . . . . . **171**
Maintaining Positive Green Habits . . . . . . . . . . . . . . . . . . . . 172
Putting It All Together (and Being Recognized) . . . . . . . . . . . 172
Staying on Top of Your Industry News . . . . . . . . . . . . . . . . . 173
Setting Up Your Benchmarks . . . . . . . . . . . . . . . . . . . . . . . . 174
The Future of Green . . . . . . . . . . . . . . . . . . . . . . . . . . . . . . . 175

*Appendix*
**Green Business Resources** . . . . . . . . . . . . . . . . . . . . . . . . . **179**
Green Resource Websites . . . . . . . . . . . . . . . . . . . . . . . . . . . 179

▲

Our 22 Green Business Examples ..................... 181

Business Resources .................................. 182

Office Supplies ..................................... 185

## Glossary ............................................. 187

## Index ................................................. 191

# Acknowledgments

I want to recognize a number of people who were very helpful in the writing of this book. Thank you to Kirstin Sanders of Orca Communications, LLC for helping me find some of the many up and coming green entrepreneurs out there. I also want to thank Jennifer Doob from Wild Dill; Shawna Pierson and Chris Kodama from iTySE; Jan and Dean McCabe from Montana Stones; Shelley Hiestand from Electric Body; Chrys Hutchings from Eco-luxury fur; Carolyn Deal from Sum-Bo-Shine; Barry Reifman from OdorZout; Sally Shepard from Shepard Public Relations; Nell Newman from Newman's Own

Organics; Mark A. Regier, Stewardship Investing Services Manager for MMA; Bill Reilly, Marketing Director for Microsoft Small and Midsized Businesses; Nick Przybyciel from Weber Shandwick Public Relations; Joshua Scott Onysko from Pangea Organics; Thanh Hua from Selfish Box; Daniel Kennedy from Chokola'j; Dan and Tina Garrido from INU Treats; Paul McGrath from RideSpring, Inc.; Kelly LaPlante from Kelly LaPlante Organic Interior Design, Inc.; Aaron Levinthal from Green Event Production and GreeNow; Folake Kuye from WeWe Clothing; Anne Bedarf from GreenBlue.org; author Trish Riley; Karel J. Samsom PhD; Chris Bartle from both The Evergreen Group LLC and Green Key Real Estate; Don Droppo from Curtis Packaging; Roger Strong from Solar Wind Works; Alex Szabo from The GreenOffice.com; David Anderson from Greenoptions.com; Kate Torgerson from Clif Bar Public Relations; my wonderful editor Courtney Thurman; and, of course, the one and only Jere Calmes from Entrepreneur Press.

# Preface

Every day, thousands, perhaps even millions, of people come up with new business ideas. There are restaurants they would love to open, shops they'd enjoy owning, and all sorts of high-tech companies that they wish they could start. Would-be inventors have ideas for time-saving inventions and artists dream of using their talents rather than working nine to five for someone else. Unfortunately not everyone is in a position to take the risk and become an entrepreneur. For some it is simply not practical with mouths to feed and bills to pay, while for others there is just too much at stake to take such a chance.

Then there are those who have the opportunity to make a go of it. Perhaps it is someone young and ambitious with few responsibilities and no family to take care of. Maybe it's a stay-at-home parent who has the extra time and funding to make a go of a new business while taking care of a young one. It might be a husband and wife who have worked long and hard to save up and strike out on their own; or a couple that has retired from their long careers and wants to start afresh in their own enterprise. The point is, there are many people from many different life situations who are enthusiastic about opening a business. If that is you, don't be frightened off by new business success and failure rates. Instead, be enthusiastic and prepared to work long and hard to make your dream of being a business owner a reality.

Owning a business isn't easy, but can be very rewarding, especially if it is a business that also represents your personal passion for the planet and the environment. Green businesses are cropping up all over the country and around the world, while established businesses do their part to make the necessary changes and improvements to get in step with the times. Today, not only can you satisfy that dream of running a business, but you can make a difference at the same time . . . and that's what this book is all about.

In the next 11 chapters you will learn about both opening a business as well as doing it with a green flair. We'll compare business names and green business names, hiring quality employees and hiring green-minded quality employees, necessary business equipment and supplies and green business equipment and supplies, marketing and promoting your business and green marketing and promoting. The point is, while it is unlikely that you will be able to start off 100 percent green, we'll discuss a variety of business areas and include the green versions throughout. In addition, we'll look at green companies of various sizes from which you can research, explore, and learn.

So, be prepared to be not only an entrepreneur, but a green entrepreneur. It's not as difficult as you might think.

# 1

# What Does "Green" Mean?

Green. It's the color of the trees, grass, plants, many vegetables, and now the term being used to describe those who are taking the environmental concerns of our planet to heart and trying to make a difference. Yes, green is now the buzzword for focusing attention on sustainability and the preservation of the environment. It is a term being used universally to indicate that you have some understanding of global warming, the greenhouse effect, and how pollution to our land and our water is endangering the planet as we know it . . . along with its inhabitants. Therefore, as Kermit the Frog used to say, "It's good to be green."

So what can you do, as a soon-to-be entrepreneur? First, you can start your business, any business, as a green business. And that's what this book is about, incorporating the environmental green into your plans and hopes of making the other green . . . money. Of course to do this your first step is to understand that the overall goal isn't just to plant trees, save water, or eat organic foods, but to recognize that Earth's bounties are being used up at a rate that is dangerous for the next generation. While science has found ways to extend life, at the same time we have also jeopardized the environment in which we can survive. Being green, or sustainable, therefore means giving back what is being taken from the earth, replenishing and respecting the planet rather than simply take from it. In a nutshell, that is what it means to be green.

## Footprints in Carbon

One of the first things you will want to do once you get your business off and running is to calculate your carbon footprint. This means seeing how much greenhouse gas emission, or $CO_2$, is the result of your company doing business as usual. By aiming to be carbon neutral, you are essentially saying that you have zero emissions through activities or are offsetting those you do have. A company's carbon imprint can be determined and measured by calculating specific information about emissions from factories, machinery, and vehicles used within the course of doing business.

You'll find several carbon calculators available online at:

○ Environmental Protection Agency: epa.gov
○ Greenhouse Gas Protocol: ghgprotocol.org
○ The Nature Conservancy: nature.org
○ Carbonfund: carbonfund.org/site/pages/carbon_calculators

## Looking Forward and Looking Back

To start a new business means to be forward thinking. Your goal is to turn a profit and grow in the coming years. With that in mind, this book will not present the detailed picture of the environmental problems that we face today. Global warming, the greenhouse effect, pollution, the disappearing forests, and other global issues have been greatly reported and highly publicized. Thus, rather than recap all of these issues, this book is designed to allow you to go forward and take the necessary measures to make a difference by running your business in a green manner, while also selling and/or manufacturing green products. Of course, throughout the book, you will see reminders of what has been done in the past, from which we need to learn. As we have progressed as a highly industrialized, highly technical society, we have also endangered the earth around us. Therefore, it is important to remember that the earth was here long before the latest and greatest technological advancements. It has withstood dinosaurs, the Ice Age, countless natural disasters, disco, and a wide variety of technical advancements in every generation. The earth has survived because it was designed to be sustainable. It is the smart entrepreneur, in any business, who recognizes that in the overall scheme of things, his or her technology is no match for the power and possibilities that mother earth has to offer. The simple reality is that you will find ecosystems existing on our earth that, without disruption from humans, can, and have, thrived for millions of years.

To move forward, it is important to step back and recognize the power available from Earth, which continues to spin, turning day into night and changing seasons on a regular schedule—even when your state-of-the-art, top-of-the-line, brand-new computer system goes down.

# Sustainability

One of the most important concepts to understand, and one of the primary definitions of a green business, is striving for sustainability. Sustainability can be defined as a process of maintaining a lifecycle at a certain level indefinitely. The idea being that the lifecycle goes from nature back to nature. In other words, what comes from the earth is tutilized in such a way as to replenish itself.

The concern today is that the modern industrialized society is preventing the earth's ability to function in a sustainable manner, disrupting ecological support systems. For a business to be sustainable, there needs to be a conscientious effort on the part of the owner(s) to set up means of supporting the environmental systems as they pertain to air, water, soil, agriculture, and forests, all of which play a part in the survival of humans and wildlife. While there is no single standardized definition of what makes a sustainable business model, the Evergreen Group, a San Francisco-based green brokerage business helping green business owners sell their businesses to like-minded buyers, provides the following:

*A sustainable business is one that operates in an environmentally responsible way. Its products and business processes are such that no negative environmental impact is felt as a result of its existence.*

Another way of looking at business from a sustainability perspective is to run your company in such a way that if it shut down tomorrow, or at any time, there would be no negative trace in the environment that it had ever been there, meaning it left no physical mark.

Of course running a 100 percent sustainable business is almost impossible, considering that products and even services take material goods into account and they need to be created, transported and distributed in some manner that usually requires some degree of technology, even if it is rudimentary or minimal. Therefore, you will see businesses with their own degree of sustainability, from old-line companies that are completely unaware of, and not focusing on, sustainability as an issue to companies that will only focus on eco-friendly means of producing, packaging, and selling products. Your hope is to be closer to the latter group, making sustainability a top priority.

For your purposes, you will need to consider:

- Your specific business needs
- Sustainable business practices
- Ways in which you can integrate the two as much as possible

For example, your business will need office equipment and supplies. You want to be sustainable, so you can look at buying recyclable and/or reusable equipment and supplies as well as utilizing them in such a manner that does not waste energy.

One of the problems faced over the last 50 years, as the United States has grown as an industrial giant in the post World War II era, has been that few companies have focused on managing waste and preserving the environment around them in what is now being called an environmentally friendly manner.

Yes, pollution in the skies has long been an issue, and government restrictions were placed on companies, but this was a mere slap on the wrist in comparison to the vast amount of waste that was accumulating in our waterways and in landfill. In fact, it was once a point of boasting that an entire building or even community was built on landfill. Of course few people would want to buy a home on such a toxic area today.

> ## Smart Tip
> Did you know that recycled paper uses close to half of the energy and as much as 90 percent less water to make paper than virgin timber, or trees cut down for the express purpose of making paper? Unfortunately, still only about 10 percent of paper used in the United States for printing is recycled.

To put it simply, sustainability is now, in large part, a response to the significant errors of the past. And while it will take active measures, such as replanting forests and cleaning out waterways and the surrounding areas to rectify this predicament, the hope of any sustainable business is *not* to add to the already existing problems caused by global industrialization.

Three keys to keep in mind when focusing on sustainability, are reducing, reusing, and recycling.

1. *Reducing*. As a new business owner, you have nothing you can reduce. The concept, however, is to use less energy and have less impact upon the environment than "traditional" businesses. What you can do, is look at the energy expenditure of businesses similar to yours and the manner in which they use natural resources and then try to limit your usage so that it is below those levels. Additionally, reducing can be as simple as not printing e-mails and thus reducing paper use.

2. *Reusing*. By taking the concept of reusing what is already available, you can minimize new production of materials, thus limiting energy expenditure and waste. Most man-made energy sources as well as many culled from the earth (such as oil), result in emitting carbon dioxide and other toxins in our air and water. This is one of the primary reasons for minimizing energy usage. Minimizing waste is necessary largely because we are simply running out of room. Products that end up in landfill can remain there for literally hundreds, if not thousands, of years, also polluting the environment. Reusing items means extending their lifetime and giving them a valuable purpose rather than serving as landfill.

3. *Recycling*. Like reusing, this is a means of utilizing products for a longer timeframe, only in this case, in a different form. Plastics, paper, and other materials can be recycled and the properties within then can continue to be of use and value. There are numerous recycling centers. It is important for business owners to learn what can and cannot be easily recycled and to set up a means of collecting recyclable items and taking them to, or having them picked up by, a recycling center.

## Dollar Stretcher

Numerous items can be reused. For example, if you do not need to use the very latest in software programs, you can reuse a computer that was formerly used by another business owner. Also keep in mind that you can reuse shipping containers and packaging that comes in for your next outgoing shipment. Boxes can also be used for planters and old crates can hold files. Be creative and reuse wherever you can.

# The Eco-Lifecycle of a Product

One way to figure out how to minimize waste and to be as environmentally responsible as possible is to trace the cycle of the products you are manufacturing, or selling, from beginning to end. This means evaluating where the materials or chemicals within a product originate, what processes are used to create products, how they are sent or shipped to you, what you do with them to prepare them for sale, how they are packaged for sale, and what happens to them through their use by the consumer. And, finally (very important), what happens to them after they have been used. How are they discarded? Are they recycled so that they can be useful again?

A very basic example could be the process of selling milk. Cows produce milk after giving birth. The milk is then collected by the farmer through a milking machine and transported as raw milk by truck to a processing plant where it is tested for bacteria and then pasteurized at temperatures of 177 degrees Fahrenheit. During this process, butterfat is then skimmed from the milk and then mixed back into the milk at different proportions, differentiating whole, skim, 1%, and 2% milk. Following homogenization, the milk is stored and cooled in tanks. It is then put into bottles or cartons and shipped to stores by refrigerated trucks. Milk is then put into refrigerators in the store, where it is purchased by consumers. After finishing the product, the carton or bottle can then be transported to a recycling plant where it can be used for another purpose.

From this basic concept, you can research each step of the process. For example, you can find out what the farmer feeds the cows; what if any chemicals are used in the pasteurization; where the bottles or cartons come from and how they are manufactured. You can also focus on the shipping of the empty and, later, full cartons and bottles as well as the transport of the milk. Once upon a time, milk was transported by horse and buggy. Today it requires trucks that use fossil fuels (bad for the environment). However, today's milk can be more thoroughly screened and bacteria can be more easily detected (good for your health). The point is, there is a story behind every product you make or sell and a story that doesn't end with the sale, but concludes with what happens to the waste materials, which in this case are cartons and bottles. If these are not recycled, or the milk is in a non-recyclable type of plastic container, then the container ends up as landfill.

So what can you do to enhance this lifecycle process?

In the above scenario, you could try several options including:

1. Look for farms and processing plants in an area near your location to minimize transport (and support local growers).
2. Look for packaging such as the bottles and/or cartons that is recyclable.

3. Look for organic farms where there are no pesticides or chemicals used.
4. Make sure consumers know that the bottles and cartons are recyclable.
5. Store milk in refrigerators powered by renewable energy sources, such as solar or wind turbine power.

The point is, with any product that you sell or manufacture you can look for ways in which that product, through its entire lifecycle, can be created, shipped, used, and discarded in an environmentally favorable manner. Learn as much as you can about what is behind the products that you sell, much in the way that Wal-Mart is doing by insisting that their vendors meet certain requirements and that packaging also meets specific criteria.

Finally, starting a business today means you should also be socially responsible. If, for example, you are importing products or parts for production from overseas, find out how the workers are treated and if they are receiving fair wages. Even locally, you'll want to know the conditions under which workers are growing, creating, packaging, and/or shipping products. Your own workers also need to be treated in a dignified and professional manner and you need to heed all employment laws, such as minimum wage and overtime laws. Social responsibility will be discussed in more detail later.

Clearly, your first objective is to get a business up and running. This may preclude you from exploring each step in the lifecycle process. However, if you want to stay in step with the concerns and issues of your consumer market, you should focus attention to some degree on the lifecycle chain. Do your homework. Environmentally aware consumers and numerous watchdog groups are doing theirs.

**Tip...**

**Smart Tip**
Know your employment law. There are plenty of books and websites on employment law. Before hiring any type of workers, make sure you are aware of the basic hiring, firing, overtime, minimum wage, discrimination, and tax laws that pertain to your employees. One place to start is the Department of Labor website at dol.gov. BusinessTown.com also has plenty of information under their "Legal" heading (business town.com).

# The Green Mindset

Having the green mindset is a marvelous place to start. If you focus your attention on starting a green business from the beginning, it will accompany you as you work through the various aspects and many tasks involved in launching a business.

There is a tremendous amount of material published in books and magazine, as well as on internet sites such as Treehugger.com and Greenbusinessalliance.com, that can put you in the right mindset based on the reality of what has been, and continues to be, a very troubling global situation. What stops many entrepreneurs from focusing on "green" is the notion that, as a small business owner, there is very little that they can do. But while it is true that you will not make the same impact upon the earth as a multi-billion dollar corporation, your business can make a difference. If you consider that 80 percent of the businesses in the United States are small to midsize their owners can and will make a significant difference if they unite. The key is getting on board from the beginning, if for no one else, for your customers or clients, many of whom are becoming environmentally savvy and want to deal with businesses that believe as they do. Surveys routinely show that more and more people are doing business with companies that have similar beliefs to their own and that environmental and socially responsible companies are reaping greater rewards.

Here are some ideas to help get you motivated:

1. *Find a green competitive edge.* It is always to your benefit to have a competitive edge, something that will help you stand out from your competitors. Look for that edge to be "green." If, for example, you are a clothing retailer, along with the popular lines your competitors are also carrying, introduce clothing made from organic cottons and other, newer, eco-friendly materials. Make it part of your marketing efforts to point out that you are carrying such items. Whatever you do, look for the greener way of doing business and then let it be known that you are the eco-friendliest in your field.

2. *Hire likeminded people.* Consider bringing in people who share your interests and business ideas, but also share your passion for the environment. Hiring people with such a mindset can help you find ways to launch your business in a greener manner.

3. *Look for underachieving opportunities.* If you have not yet decided on a business, explore businesses that have not been embraced by the green mindset, or at least ones in which there is room for vast improvement. There are areas such as organic foods and cosmetics, where companies like Pangea Organics have built a strong green foundation. It is advantageous to look for industries that have, as a whole, not yet embraced "green" as much as they could. GreeNow, a New York-based company providing generators and other equipment for festivals, concerts, and events, was formed largely because the owners discovered that no other companies were providing biodiesel-powered generators or forklifts. After doing research, they found that not only could this be done and replace petroleum-based equipment, but that there was a major demand for greener ways of running such events.

4. *Learn a lot.* Start educating yourself and getting into the mindset by visiting websites such as envirolink.org, Alliance to Save Energy at ase.org, Energy Savers at energysavers.gov, Energystar.com, Treehuggers.com, Earthwatch.org, Planetgreen.com, or one of numerous other environmental websites. Turn on Planet Green TV and, if you haven't seen it, rent Al Gore's film *An Inconvenient Truth*. You will also find inspiration from reading about the green efforts of other businesses such as Timberland, Starbucks, Wal-Mart, or one of many small companies like Clif Bar, The Evergreen Group, or New Belgium Brewery that have a very green outlook. (There are nearly two dozen such green companies featured in the next chapter.)

5. *Get involved.* While starting up a business will take a great deal of your time, you might also opt to get involved in some green organizations and associations. This will allow you to both learn and meet like-minded individuals from which you can cull some ideas, both green and business. Hands-on involvement in environmental activities can be a real eye-opener. A perfect example of how such hands-on activities can lead to greener actions comes from Clif Bar Staff Ecologist Elysa Hammond. "We did a beach cleanup project as a way of getting everyone actively involved. One of the leaders of our R&D department was so affected by picking up all of the plastic and Styrofoam waste that, when he received packages with Styrofoam peanuts, he wrote back to the companies politely explaining why he would appreciate it if they would send future packaging without this plastic or Styrofoam. He explained how it affects wildlife. The result was far less plastic sent in packaging. The point being that such a project can enlighten members of your own staff and they can spread the word about their new-found knowledge through hands-on experience. After all, we typically learn a lot more when in the throes of an activity, rather than just reading about it.

# What Does a Green Office Look Like?

Desk-side recycling bins, energy-efficient lighting rather than fluorescent lighting, and plants used as natural air filters are part of the green office environment. The idea should be to minimize waste, keep energy bills low, utilize energy-efficient equipment, and enjoy both fresh air and clean air within the office.

No matter what business you are in, you can start off with some fundamentals in place, such as a waste management plan, sustainability plan, and green purchasing policy so that buying recycled products whenever possible is the norm. Starting a green business means establishing eco-friendly policies from the beginning. If you have an office that reflects your environmental concerns then you will be more inclined to operate in a green manner in all of your business dealings.

# Have You Ever Stepped Into a Green Store?

Environmentally-friendly products on the shelves, packaged in recyclable containers, reusable cloth bags on sale for a nominal fee or perhaps for free at the checkout counters, and less inventory but more options available on computers and kiosks are all part of what the environmental model of how a green retail store looks today.

Many retailers see the benefits of medium to smaller locations that require less heat in the winter and air conditioning pumping cooler air in the summer. They also see the benefits of encouraging consumers to bring their own cloth bags in which to carry goods home on a regular basis rather than the "paper or plastic" option.

Organic products, earth-friendly options, and an environment that clearly shows customers that "we care about the planet" will help you launch a green retail business.

# Have You Been to a Green Factory Lately?

Chemical free, toxin free, high indoor air quality, safety precautions in place, good natural ventilation, and products utilizing recycled and/or natrural materials with either little waste or a means of utilizing remnants from production are all part of the greener manufacturing model.

No matter what you plan to make, you can very likely find ingredients and materials that are organic, natural, nontoxic, and/or recyclable. The eco-lifecycle of the products are studied carefully to determine the best means of making, selling, and shipping products without leaving a significant carbon imprint on the earth.

# The Green Homebased Businesses . . .
# Have You Seen One?

Open windows minimize the need for air conditioning, furnishings are innovative in their use of recycled materials, and the lighting is natural from a skylight—the home office can be your personal green presentation of your business featuring eco-friendly surroundings and energy-efficient equipment. You can make the most out of that which you, or friends and neighbors, have lying around and think organic from décor to daily snacks.

While this is just a taste of the manner in which you can operate your business, it is the setting in which you can create, sell, and market your products and/or services.

# Balancing Pragmatic Business Concerns
# with an Environmental Approach

Sustainability, waste management, energy conservation, using natural resources, recycling, thinking organic, and so on. There are plenty of ways to approach being green. On the other side of the equation, you have meeting consumer demand, hiring top people, watching your costs, marketing to find new customers while keeping current ones happy, maintaining a cash flow, keeping shareholders and stakeholders content, and making a profit. These are all part and parcel of the business side of the equation.

No matter how green you want your business to be, if you are losing money, your business will not be around very long. And, if you have a true passion for helping the environment, you owe it to yourself, and the planet, to try to maintain your business as a profitable entity.

So, how do you balance the two areas, business and green?

You might liken the response to the old two step, where you take two-steps forward and one step back. This means moving ahead with your business plan in a manner that is profitable and meets your needs, while taking a step back to make sure you are incorporating green measures each step of the way . . . if possible. You will need to punch numbers and determine the cost of tradition versus greener methods of running your business. In some cases you will find that you will not be spending anything more to be green, and in fact will be saving money by recycling and reusing products.

In other areas, the cost of starting out green may be prohibitive. Keep in mind, however, that if you can get rebates and government support for building green or using renewable energy that this might also lead to a cost savings. It is important, as mentioned earlier, to know your business very well. This will allow you to make the tough decisions, such as where you may need to spend a little more now to save more money later.

Remember, you are also better starting off at 25 or 50 percent green, than not launching a profitable business. While you have an obligation to the environment, you also have an obligation to yourself, your backers, and your stakeholders to get the business off the ground and making money. You can take small steps—to paraphrase a popular saying—a journey to 100 percent carbon neutrality starts with one step in that direction. Small steps can be the beginning of much greater success. Profits can also be a means of supporting environmental causes, such as giving to One Percent for the Planet, which utilizes one percent of the profits donated from numerous businesses—large or small—to help environmental organizations worldwide, or the Conservation Alliance, which supports environmental organizations in their efforts to protect threatened wild lands.

And, if you can't afford to power all of, or most of, your facility by solar energy, you can buy carbon offsets as a means of contributing to the environment. While this is not the same as "doing your own thing" it is a way of "hopefully" making a difference. To do this, you calculate your carbon footprint, as noted earlier, and you buy offsets to reduce an equal amount of carbon somewhere else in the world through your donation. Theoretically, you want to be balancing your carbon-producing activities by lowering a carbon footprint somewhere else, or doing something beneficial elsewhere. It's almost as if you missed a day of work (seven hours) at a green company, but compensated by using one of your off-days (like a Sunday) to do something good for the environment for seven hours someplace else. Hence the principle of carbon offsets is that rather than doing something yourself, you are donating money for some organization to do the environmental work for you.

While carbon offsets are easy to purchase, you should do some research to learn how and where your money is being spent. Here are a few places to visit online to get an idea of how they use the funding from selling their carbon offsets:

- Atmosclear: atmosclear.org
- The Carbonfund: Carbonfund.org
- e-Blue Horizons: e-bluehorizons.net
- Eco2Pass: eco2pass.com
- Greenoffice: greenoffice.com
- Native Energy: nativeenergy.org
- Natsource: natsource.com

More than $100 million dollars in carbon offsets were purchased voluntarily in both 2007 and 2008. There are some countries that require businesses to buy offsets once they have reached a certain level of carbon emissions. Thus far that is not the case in the United States.

The hope is that by buying carbon offsets, your company can approach carbon neutrality. One carbon offset represents the reduction of one metric ton of carbon dioxide, or its equivalent in other greenhouse gases, such as methane.

Carbon offsets, however, should be your last option. That's right, your *last* option. This should not be a means of buying your way out of actually *being* a green company. Nor should they be bought simply to ease your conscience.

Just as supplements, diet pills, or medicines are no substitute for eating a nutritious diet and health-conscious menu choices, carbon offsets do not substitute for green practices and an eco-friendly environment. A green-business owner should be thinking of sustainable practices, recycling, reusing, saving energy, and being involved in hands-on initiatives that benefit the planet first, before looking to purchase carbon offsets.

On the positive side, carbon offsets do put money toward thousands of projects designed to reduce carbon emissions, re-plant forests, save endangered wildlife, clean up land and water, and so forth.

On the negative side, there is not much regulation of carbon offsets and no central board overseeing them. As a result, in many cases it is difficult to know if the money is being used to benefit the environment and what measures are taken in the long term to make sure that such projects will be sustained. For example, trees planted to rejuvenate a forest is a positive use of the carbon offsets. However, if there is nobody overseeing the ongoing growth of these trees, which can take many years, and they are subsequently chopped down to make paper, you are defeating the purpose of your initial plan, to re-establish the forests.

The other concern critics raise regarding carbon offsets is whether you are paying to have work done that would have been done regardless, in which case the funding is not going to anything new. "Are there additional results?" asks Anne Bedarf, Project Manager at GreenBlue.org, a Virginia-based nonprofit institute that focuses on the expertise of professional communities to create practical solutions, resources, and opportunities for implementing sustainability. In other words, is something being done that would not have been done anyway?

For more on carbon offsets, you can go to ecobusinesslinks.com and find information and prices for various carbon offsetting sellers, plus the type of offsets sold and the type of projects your money is going to support. Another website, called Cleanair-coolplanet.org also has information on the various carbon offsets that you can purchase. Again, keep in mind that while carbon offsets may very well be a step in the right direction, even if 50 percent of the funding is used to benefit the environment, buying offsets does not make a company green and should be used to balance the amount of carbon emissions that you, as a practical business owner, need to expend to maintain a successful business.

# **Business** Decisions

Starting a business means making many key decisions. First, you will need to decide on the type of business you wish to open and then on the amount of time and effort you are ready to put into a business venture. Of course, this will vary depending on your specific goals, needs, and desires. For some, the dream is to plant the seeds for a multi-billion dollar corporation while for others it is a part-time business for additional income.

Before you can start a green business, you need to be passionate about the type of business you are planning to embark upon. You need to see this as a business with the potential to make money while benefiting the environment in some manner. If you are able to launch a green business properly, whether it is a full-time or part-time venture, you want to do so in such a way that is both sustainable (eco-friendly) and profitable!

While we are not going to get into great detail on how to select among the myriad business possibilities, we will take some time to ask the pertinent questions to help you establish some clear goals. You want to have both a sense of direction from a financial perspective and one that meets your environmental concerns in keeping with your personal beliefs.

# What Are Your Personal Goals?

Starting a business has a lot to do with your personality and what you want to achieve in life. Many entrepreneurs start businesses because their goals are to work for themselves, earn a steady income to support, or help support, their families, and have the flexibility to make their own decisions and work their own hours.

Personal goals are those that affect you as an individual. They are about your dreams, desires, and ideals. For example, you may start a specific business because you enjoy being outdoors rather than cooped up in an office or because you enjoy working with your hands or want to become more physically active and fit. Many business owners today are starting businesses with the personal goal of doing something positive for the environment. Your personal goals should be based on:

- What you enjoy doing
- Where your experience/expertise lie
- What you believe in
- What provides you with a sense of personal (not financial) satisfaction
- What fits into your current lifestyle, which includes your family or life situation (For example: Are you single? Part of a two-income household? Do you have children? Are you retired from a long-time career?)

One of the nicest things about listing your personal goals before going into a business is that they cannot be wrong. They could be unrealistic, such as making enough money to save an entire rain forest, or you could be planning a business that is too small to meet the needs of your family, but they are still your dreams and aspirations, some of which may simply need to be scaled down or expanded upon for the sake of practicality.

Below you can list your personal goals, which will serve you well in deciding on a business venture or, if you have a business venture already in mind, help you plan accordingly to work toward your goals.

You will want to define both your short- and long-term personal goals, prior to starting any business. Use the worksheet below to help you recognize those goals. These may include being your own boss as well as making personally rewarding changes in your lifestyle over the years to come. While it's impossible to know what your future will hold, you can look at upcoming changes and personal life events and plan accordingly.

## Defining Your Personal Goals Worksheet

In order of priority, list your short-term (1–5 years) personal goals:

1. _____

2. _____

3. _____

4. _____

5. _____

In order of priority, list your long-term (5+ years) personal goals:

1. _____

2. _____

3. _____

4. _____

5. _____

# What Are Your Financial Goals?

A rewarding business takes on two elements: providing personal satisfaction and financial freedom. After all, if you want to be tied to someone else's personal goals or be under-compensated for your efforts, you could always work for someone else.

Therefore, your second set of goals to consider—as you embark on any type of business—are your financial goals. Are you anticipating a business that will earn you a profit of $50,000 or $250,000? Are you starting a business for a supplemental income or for your primary income? Sure, everyone starts a business with the goal of making money, but in conjunction with the above-mentioned personal goals (which put you in a business you would enjoy running) you will need to factor in a realistic amount of money with which to support yourself and/or a family. As mentioned in personal goals, the amount of income you will need will depend on your life situation. Are you the sole supporter of a family? Do you have only yourself to feed and clothe? Are you part of a two-income family (which is very common today)? Are you maintaining a "traditional" job and launching a homebased business for some extra income? Answers to these questions will determine what income level will be a realistic goal.

In addition, there are milestones and long-term goals you will need to consider when starting a business such as stashing away enough money to put the kids through college, paying off the mortgage, buying a vacation home, and amassing enough wealth on which to retire comfortably by age 55. You will want to look at and list your financial goals including putting money toward your personal beliefs in the environment and social responsibility, which today go hand-in-hand. Use the financial goals worksheet.

# What Are Your Business Goals?

Business goals center on the size, type, and structure of the business you want to start. For example, are you looking to open a health spa with 24 employees or would you prefer a three-person, very hands-on, landscaping business? Are you going to be a service provider from a homebased office, or open a tutoring service with classrooms and fifteen tutors working with students in a well-situated location? The size and type of business you open will be based largely on your resources, including how much money and manpower you have to start your business, along with your experience in the field and your ability to be a leader. Too many people want to run a large business but do not have the leadership qualities to do so. Conversely, many two-person operations could grow if the owners wanted such expansion, but they remain small because the goal was just that, a small self-contained business. Your personal and financial goals, along with your resources will play into your business goals.

## Defining Your Financial Goals Worksheet

In order of priority, list your short-term (1–5 years) financial goals:

1. _____

2. _____

3. _____

4. _____

5. _____

In order of priority, list your long-term (5+ years) financial goals:

1. _____

2. _____

3. _____

4. _____

5. _____

Therefore, once you have decided upon the type of business you wish to open, think about where you see that business in five or ten years. In other words, will your car wash be the first of three in your local area within five years and a franchise covering the entire Northeastern region of the country in ten years? Or, will you have a small car wash that simply adds other amenities and services in five years and becomes fully automated as technology advances in ten years?

The manner in which you see the business taking shape, growing, expanding, or not, is all part of your business goals. You can also determine whether you see yourself taking on 1 or 21 employees, adding new technology, and/or selling the business by the ten-year anniversary. Use the worksheet on page 20 to help you understand your business goals.

▲

## Defining Your Business Goals Worksheet

In order of priority, list your short-term (1–5 years) business goals:

1. _____

2. _____

3. _____

4. _____

5. _____

In order of priority, list your long-term (5+ years) business goals:

1. _____

2. _____

3. _____

4. _____

5. _____

# What Are Your Environmental Goals?

If you are reading a book on starting a green business, you are clearly motivated to make a positive impact on the environment. Therefore, in conjunction with your personal, financial, and business goals, you need to include your environmental goals; these will also factor in with the other three categories.

You may want to run a business with as close to a zero carbon footprint as possible, meaning you are producing a minimal amount of carbon monoxide emissions and buying carbon offsets to cover that which you do produce. Your goals may be to make a difference in the local landscape, cleaning up a neighborhood beach or park. You may want a business whereby everyone uses alternative transportation to commute to and from your office or store. You may want to educate other businesses by setting an eco-friendly example in everything you do or even providing tours of your facility to illustrate your procedures, much as New Belgium Brewery in Colorado did, inviting business leaders, to tour the greenest brewery in America . . . even the head of Wal-Mart stopped by for a lengthy visit. The point is that you can have several environmental goals. You should list them for the near and far future using the worksheet below. Perhaps by five years you will be a fully sustainable business and by ten years operate on 100 percent renewable energy. You may also want to start with initiatives that include both your employees and your community.

## Defining Your Environmental Goals Worksheet

In order of priority, list your short-term (1–5 years) environmental goals:

1. _____

2. _____

3. _____

4. _____

5. _____

In order of priority, list your long-term (5+ years) environmental goals:

1. _____

2. _____

3. _____

4. _____

5. _____

▲

# How to Choose the Right Business

A green business is one of your primary goals. However, to get there, you need to determine what type of business you want to pursue. The three broad categories of businesses are those that:

1. Sell products
2. Sell services
3. Manufacture products

Of course there are plenty of businesses that do all three, or two out of three. For example, you may be a manufacturer of eco-friendly kitchen cabinets made with FSC (Forest Stewardship Council) certified woods, sell them at your showroom, and also do installation and repairs on such cabinets, providing the manufacturing, sales, and service aspects. You will need a level of expertise in each area to make such a business work. After all, if you can make the cabinets, but are terrible at sales, your business will be in trouble. You could always decide to have other dealerships and kitchen stores do the selling for you. The point is, assess what you can do well and go from there.

Let's look at the three key ingredients: sales, manufacturing, and service.

## Are You Inclined to Sell?

While you need not be an outgoing "in your face" salesperson, to go into selling, whether it is retail sales in a store, via the internet, through catalogs, at trade shows, or by appointment only (wholesale or retail) you do need to have some expertise in one or more types of products and be able to discern the means of buying, marking up, and selling. At the most basic level, selling means meeting a demand with a supply. This is not always easy, and may take marketing, promotion, advertising, and convincing people that they need what you have to sell. People in sales work long and hard to analyze their product(s) and those of their competitors, so being an expert in that which you are selling certainly helps.

Anyone opening a sales-oriented business needs to learn how to make a product seem most appealing and marketable (or hire salespeople who have that knack). There are many books and articles written about what it takes to excel at sales. Confidence in your product(s), good listening skills so that you hear what your customers want, and the ability to solve their needs are three key ingredients along with knowing how to close a sale and when "no" means "no."

Green products today are those that save energy, prevent unnecessary waste, are recyclable, reusable, nontoxic, organic, and/or otherwise not harmful to the planet.

These qualifications are major selling points unto themselves. Doing market research, you will find that a growing percentage of your potential buying market is concerned with the environment, which bodes well for selling environmentally safe versions of almost any product. And with few exceptions, you can find eco-friendly adaptations of almost anything.

If you are thinking of a sales-oriented green business, ask yourself:

- Am I a people person?
- Am I good with numbers (for inventory, pricing, and determining a profit margin)?
- Do I have a knack for accentuating the positives of products or services?
- Am I a good listener?
- Am I comfortable selling, or should I find people who are?
- Do I have an interest in (and some expertise in) a particular product or industry (such as sporting goods, women's apparel, or medical supplies)?
- Can I seek out and find the green versions of products that I want to sell?
- Can I sell greener products than my competition?

## Can You Provide a Service?

From consultants to decorators to dentists to landscape architects, if there is a skill you possess, and/or a license or degree you hold verifying your ability in an area of expertise, you can open a service-based business. The key elements to a service business are:

- Knowing your capabilities
- Knowing what services people want and what they expect
- Scheduling your time and pricing yourself accordingly.

Even if you do not personally have such a skill, you could run a service-oriented business by hiring those individuals who do possess the abilities that are wanted and/or needed by a target market. From tutoring to escorts to auto detailers to party planners to photographers, you can send the people who provide services to clients while you serve as the organizer, scheduler, and business owner.

A green service business takes into consideration the tools of the trade, the location in which a service is performed and the necessary commuting. In some instances you may be able to minimize your impact on the planet through the service being performed. For example, a good green architect or landscaper today can have various strategies for building a greener home or planting and maintaining a thriving garden.

If you are thinking of a service-oriented green business, ask yourself:

- Am I a people person?
- Am I good with organization and scheduling?
- Do I have a marketable service/skill that I can perform?
- Do I have credibility (through certifications, licensing, etc.)?
- Can I find and/or manage others with service experience?
- Can I market this service to a defined target audience?
- Can this service help create a greener environment or can it be performed in a green manner?

## Into Manufacturing?

The third type of business is manufacturing, which can include making anything from children's toys to rocket ships. While some products are made to fill a void in a market, many entrepreneurs open manufacturing facilities because they have ideas and plans to make a better product or a familiar product in a different manner than those already widely available. An entrepreneur in the business of manufacturing any type of product needs to be well versed in the details of the product his or her company will be producing and the public's need for the product.

Manufacturing greener products means that you will study and include environmentally friendly materials and create, grow, or assemble them in an eco-friendly manner. In addition, you will use manufacturing processes that do not result in waste and/or pollution of the air or water. And finally, shipping and transport needs should be considered in a green manufacturing business.

If you are thinking of a manufacturing business, ask yourself:

- Is there a product or line of products that I feel strongly about making?
- Do I have expertise in creating and/or manufacturing a product?
- Do I have innovative ideas that I can train people to produce?

> **Beware!**
> There are service providers and so-called service providers. While it is illegal to practice some services, such as those in the medical and legal field, without a license, there are various levels of consultants and advisors out there who only marginally fit the criteria. Unlike a product that is tangible, a service is only as good as the service provider. Therefore, if you are hiring anyone from a masseuse to a chef, make sure whomever is performing a service in your business has credible references and a background that suits your needs and degree of experience. Service industries are very dependant on their reputation.

- Do I have confidence (from market research) that this is a product the public will want, need, and buy?
- Am I good with numbers to determine the cost for making products and the profit margin for selling them?
- Can I find greener ways of making "traditional" products?
- Can I find greener means of packaging and shipping products?
- Can I provide greener alternatives by making a recyclable or reusable product?

Another potential business not mentioned here would be farming and agriculture. In a broad sense, these are essentially manufacturing products by way of growing them, as is the case with food or plants.

Sales and marketing skills also need to be addressed in order to move what you grow. Organically grown produce is clearly another green option, depending on your interest in, passion for, and knowledge of agriculture.

# Suit Yourself

The key is to find a business that suits your passions, personality, strengths, experience, goals, beliefs, and ideals. When you stop to think about how much time you will be putting into a business, you really want to get something back for all of that effort, besides the obvious, money.

Clearly, there is much more to consider when embarking on a new business. According to noted professor, consultant, and ecologist Karel J. Samsom, PhD, from his paper "The 4 E's: Entrepreneurship, Economy, Ecology, and the Ego!":

Entrepreneurs need not be weighted down by the cultural or monetary habits of "the business culture as usual." Solo entrepreneurs and new ventures offer unique capabilities to create value. This is especially true in an age where economic activity increasingly exceeds the physical limitations of what the ecology of the Earth can support or absorb. When the physical impact of economic activity continuously exceeds the ability of the ecology of the Earth to absorb and recover, an impossible situation arises which leads to either borrowing resources from following generations and/or polluting the current inhabitants of the Earth. Thus, one of the key success drivers for green businesses is to understand this connection between economy and ecology and consciously use the practical implications thereof in designing all marketing tools.

Along with the marketing tools that Dr. Samsom mentions, designing and creating a business that, at all levels, taps into green innovations and processes can serve as a model for other businesses while providing an entrepreneur with rewards far greater than those that are monetary.

# There's No Need to Re-Invent the Wheel: A Look at 22 Successful Green Businesses

Sure, you've read about Starbucks, Wal-Mart, and Timberland all making great strides to go greener. Many established businesses are working hard to move in the eco-friendly direction with excellent results. However, there are also numerous small businesses that started with an environmental, "green," mindset; they can serve as role models for entrepreneurs such as yourself, who are just launching their businesses.

Below are 22 of the many examples of businesses that have embraced the green philosophy from the start. They range from some small businesses that have grown substantially to brand new two-person operations. Their revenues and profit margins vary greatly, as do their products and services, which range from organic pet foods to pizza. They do, however, share a common goal: to benefit the planet and the health of those inhabiting it.

You can use these as examples from which to cull ideas of practical applications when designing and starting your own company, or you can simply read about them to reaffirm your belief that a business with an environmental, sustainable mission is not only possible but can be highly successful. So I present the following list of 22 green business examples (in no particular order).

## 1. Pangea Organics
### pangeaorganics.com

Pangea was designed from the outset to be a sustainable company and now sports a zero carbon footprint. Along with creating and selling original organic skincare products, their packaging is made from a zero waste process featuring 100 percent post-consumer paper and organic seeds such as sweet basil and amaranth. This allows the consumer to return the box to the environment by removing the label, soaking it in water for a minute and planting it back into the earth. Speaking of the earth, Pangea Organics also supports women-owned farms. According to founder and president Joshua Onysko, "87 percent of the world's food is grown by women and they own 1 percent of the world's land, so we are hoping to finance women-owned farms in countries that produce some of our raw materials. We're hoping by 2012 that 20 percent of our ingredients will be produced by women-owned farms that we supported and helped to grow."

## 2. Patagonia
### patagonia.com

Since the 1970s this outdoor clothing and gear manufacturer has been a leader in sustainability. Patagonia was one of the first companies to use organic cotton and recycled plastic fleece. They have continued to introduce innovative environmentally friendly materials over their long history. Along with recycling old clothing, using only recycled paper in their marketing and catalogs, and powering buildings with renewable energy, Patagonia also leads environmental and conservation efforts.

They have given more than $31 million dollars to numerous organizations active in protecting the environment, wilderness, and promoting biodiversity. In addition, Patagonia co-founded The Conservation Alliance in 1989. The alliance unites like-minded companies in the outdoors industry in order to support environmental efforts and to protect endangered wildlife and land.

## 3. New Belgium Brewery
### newbelgium.com

Husband and wife Jeff Lebish and Kim Jordan hiked up into the mountains to sit quietly and determine how to take their home brewing and create a full working brewery that would be good to the environment. Apparently, they came up with an excellent plan. The Colorado-based company became the first beer maker to power all of its operations with wind turbine power. The company also opted to fuel all of their trucks with biodiesel and treat wastewater on site, resulting in a dramatic reduction in water usage. In addition, New Belgium manages several acres of land and provides other companies with waste products that are used for other purposes such as fish food. Strong supporters of alternative, eco-friendly means of commuting, New Belgium gives each employee a bicycle after one year of work. They also support and sponsor a number of biking events and even have bike-in movies, using the old drive-in concept of showing an outdoor movie, but they take place on the lawn for people showing up by bike.

## 4. Clif Bar & Company
### clifbar.com

This Berkeley, California-based business is one of the most notable eco-friendly companies on the planet. Clif Bar makes a variety of healthy organic snack bars using primarily organic products. In addition, they use recycled paper and nontoxic inks on their packaging, which is all eco-friendly. By moving their distribution centers and switching to sustainable biodiesel in their trucks, Clif Bar & Company have lowered their carbon footprint by minimizing inter-company shipping from bakeries to distribution centers. In fact, they went from using 508 tons of $CO2$ in 2003 to 15 tons in 2007. Along with their products, packaging, and shipping, Clif Bar is very active in a vast number of environmental activities and with numerous well-known charitable groups and organizations. Their monthly newsletter highlights many hands-on campaigns, fundraisers, and activities that staff members have been involved in, along with the community. A well-rounded pragmatic and socially conscious business, Clif Bar lists five aspirations to which they adhere: Sustaining Our Planet, Sustaining Our Community, Sustaining Our People, Sustaining Our Business, and Sustaining Our Brands.

## 5. Green Mountain Coffee Roasters
### greenmountaincoffee.com

Based in the mountains of Vermont, Green Mountain Coffee Roasters opened in 1981 and went public on the NASDAQ in 1993. During that time, and ever since, they have been committed to creating and selling more than 100 high-quality coffee selections while maintaining their model of sustainability, which placed them on SustainableBusiness.com's 2007 list of The World's Top 20 Sustainable Business Stocks.

The core values of Green Mountain have long been to protect the environment and to focus on waste reduction and responsible energy use. From composting in the early days to establishing an employee Environment Committee in 1989, there have been many activities and initiatives launched to better the planet. Earth-friendly coffee filters were soon followed by the first biodegradable coffee bag for bulk purchases in the 1990s. More recently, in 2006, the company introduced the ecotainer™, the world's first to-go cup for hot beverages made entirely out of renewable materials.

Green Mountain is constantly at the forefront of innovation when it comes to eco-friendly products. In addition, they have worked with Root Capital to provide millions of dollars in loans to cash-strapped coffee farmers.

## 6. Kettle Foods
### kettlefoods.com

Featuring award-winning all-natural chips with no trans fats and no MSG, this Oregon-based food maker has grown into a leading eco-friendly company. Along with making chips using sunflower and safflower oils, Kettle runs a fleet of vehicles powered by distilled vegetable oil. In fact, 100 percent of the waste vegetable oil from the chips is converted into biodiesel fuel.

A leader in renewable energy, Kettle has 600 solar panels set on roof-mounted racks, which generate enough power to make 250,000 bags of chips and reduce the company's annual $CO_2$ emissions by 65 tons. In addition, Kettle, which has been recognized by the Environmental Protection Agency's Green Power Partnership, has purchased enough wind energy credits to thwart more than 12 million pounds of carbon dioxide pollution.

Kettle also sports wind turbines on their roof and brings in nearly 40 percent of their building materials from within a 500-mile radius of a projected building, thus mitigating the $CO_2$ emissions of numerous trucks.

# 7. Seventh Generation
## seventhgeneration.com

Starting as a small Vermont-based green company, Seventh Generation has, in 20 years, established itself as a leader in the green cleaning industry. Committed from day one to a passion for saving natural resources and reducing pollution, Seventh Generation created a line of nontoxic household products that includes non-chlorine bleached, 100 percent recycled paper towels, bathroom and facial tissues, and napkins; nontoxic, phosphate-free cleaning, dish and laundry products; plastic trash bags made from recycled plastic; chlorine-free baby diapers, training pants, and baby wipes; and chlorine-free feminine care products, including organic cotton tampons.

Seventh Generation also partnered with a number of organizations including Balle (aka The Business Alliance for Local Living Economies), Grassroots.org, and Healthy Child Healthy World, which is dedicated to protecting children from harmful environmental exposures.

# 8. Pizza Fusion
## pizzafusion.com

Yes, pizza places can be green too. Pizza Fusion, originally based in Fort Lauderdale, Florida, specializes in organic pizzas and has expanded to more than 50 locations in seven states. The two originators, college buddies Michael Gordon and Vaughan Lazar, were determined to start a business that featured great-tasting pizza while at the same time being beneficial to the planet. With that in mind, they opted to buy a fleet of hybrid vehicles to bring pizzas in recyclable boxes to customer's homes, using minimal $CO_2$ emissions. They also knew that happy employees would benefit their mission, so for any employee working over a 20-hour week, they offered a health plan. Finally, once the concept was a hit, they decided to start franchising, but only in stores that met LEED (Leadership in Energy and Environmental Design) standards and were powered with 100 percent wind energy. Any additional power is offset by the purchase of renewable wind energy credits. All of this is in keeping with their motto, "Saving the Earth, One Pizza at a Time."

## 9. The Evergreen Group LLC and Green Key Real Estate

### greenkeyrealestate.com

Housed in one San Francisco carbon neutral office, complete with Energy Star appliances and plenty of recycled paper, are two businesses owned by the same entrepreneur. For the past seven years, the Evergreen Group has been selling small green businesses to likeminded buyers. Green Key Real Estate, just three years old, has recently begun franchising with a green business model. They handle primarily residential property and small-scale mixed use properties. "As we get bigger we will be building relationships with developers who are doing green projects and at that point set up sales offices and really work on larger projects," explains founder and CEO Chris Bartle.

While there is no one definition of "green" real estate, Bartle explains that Green Key looks for certification, such as FSC-certified building materials and homes rated by Green Point, which is part of the California Program, Building Green.

The green real estate business is also about homes in which sellers have included green features and/or homes where buyers are looking to add green features. Bartle points to three main categories for green real estate. "Energy efficiency, indoor air quality [which means using nontoxic materials and finishes], and water conservation are all taken into account," says Bartle, who runs the first green real estate franchise of its kind.

## 10. Solar Wind Works

### solarwindworks.com

A full-service renewable energy business, the Truckee, California-based company handles all aspects of wind turbine power. Owner Chris Worchester serves as an example of what can be done, living off-grid for the past 20 years. The epitome of green expertise, Solar Wind Works guide their clients through the process from conception to installation. They also know their products, which include wind energy products, solar PV products, solar hot water products, DC to AC power inverters, charge controllers, renewable energy system batteries, hybrid power systems, generators, and more. "For solar energy, we utilize solar maps of the United States, which illustrate areas of lower and higher sun ratings," explains Roger Strong, a renewable-energy consultant for Solar Wind Works. They have a similar means of measuring wind power for wind turbines.

Sporting numerous certifications, Solar Wind Works is a green business dedicated to helping local businesses and home owners experience a greener way of life.

## 11. WeWe Clothing
### weweclothing.com

As you might imagine, this is clothing primarily for little tikes, and some for older kids (plus a few things for grown ups too!) made primarily from organic materials. The homebased business in Beverly Hills, California, was started by clothing designer Folake Kuye, who wanted out of the nine-to-five routine and into a manageable business, where her husband helped by setting up the website. The business is almost entirely paperless and the husband-and-wife team work hard to recycle, save energy, and use means of alternative transportation for errands and any business needs, which includes not only bikes, but the occasional skateboard. The website also has eco-recommendations such as saving water and energy by washing clothes by hand.

## 12. Newman's Own Organics
### newmansownorganics.com

Nell Newman, the daughter of Paul Newman and Joanne Woodward, started her organic food business back in 1993, when even the mention of organic foods raised eyebrows. "People back east, where I grew up, thought I was nuts," says Nell, who launched her organic food business under the Newman food umbrella. In fact, it was dad's food business that was the catalyst for Newman's Own Organics. "Dad's favorite snack was pretzels when I was growing up, so we thought we would start with that as our first product," explains Nell, who found a small pretzel manufacturing plant that was willing to bring in flour in bags and create the organic version of pretzels. From that initial offering, some 15 years later the company has grown to include chocolate bars, Fig Newmans, Pop's Corn, Champion chip cookies, Soy Crisps, mints, caramel butter cups, their own delicious peanut butter cups, coffee, tea, and more. There's even a line of organic pet foods. The success of Newman's Own Organics is based largely on the commitment to selling organic foods that rival any traditional offerings in taste while being much healthier. Newman, who took the time to research and study the way in which food is grown and marketed adds that, "If people only knew what went into traditional foods, everyone would be buying organic."

# 13. Odorzout
## odorzout.com or 88stink.com

Unlike Superman, who fears Kryptonite, Dr. Stink absolutely loves Zeolites, in fact, it's the mineral behind his success. No, we're not talking about a comic book hero, but the man behind Odorzout, which features all natural products that eliminate odors. Some 15 years ago, Barry Reifman (aka Dr. Stink) learned of Zeolites from a geologist friend and he was launched into a green business before "green" was in fashion. Today, Odorzout not only has a host of natural products that take the odor out of everything from cat litter to laundry, but it is the all-natural odor eliminating product that has been given the EPA's "Designed for the Environment" seal of approval. In addition, Odorzout also sports the National Health & Wellness Club's seal of approval on their Laundry Additive. The all-natural odor eliminator does not mask, cover up, or perfume, but instead absorbs and eliminates odors. Dressed in his green lab coat, Dr. Stink tells potential customers more about the amazing green products at commercial and trade shows. In addition, the packaging and even the labels are all recyclable. Products are now carried by some major players including PetSmart, Tru Value Hardware, Ace Hardware Arizona, and Whole Food Arizona.

# 14. Inu Treats
## inutreats.com

Dan and Tina Garrido got the idea for starting a business that sells all natural holistic treats for the modern pet when they learned that one of their own two dogs had allergies. "After all of the pet food recalls in 2007, we wanted to make something that was healthy for animals and made from natural ingredients," says Dan of their initial concept, which began with four products in fun shapes. Using natural and some organic ingredients, the husband-and-wife team did their test marketing at street fairs in the Seattle area and altered the ingredients depending on the reaction they were getting from pet owners, and ultimately the pets themselves. Pretty soon, a couple of stores wanted to buy and distribute the product. After one year, 200 stores are now part of the Inu distribution channels, which has also expanded into Canada and Asia.

Now in an 8,000-square-foot factory, the pet treat business is thriving in a green environment. "We try to use all recycled products and we use soy ink on business cards. Our packaging also has a paragraph on the company's commitment to being earth friendly," adds Dan, who also works with a green marketing company to spread the word about healthy pet snacks from Inu Treats.

# 15. GreeNow
## greenow.org

Some businesses emerge because they meet a demand. That's the case with GreeNow, making events of all kinds, including festivals, concerts, and corporate outings greener by powering them with biodiesel rather than petroleum. Aaron Levinthal, who has his own production company and has been in the event business for 15 years, was asked frequently by planners how they could make their events greener, beyond using recyclable cups and plates. "I thought about it and realized that power was probably the biggest abuser of the environment, between forklifts and generators used at such events," explains Levinthal, who proceeded to ask the companies that rent generators if they could use biodiesel. "I got a resounding 'no' across the board," says Levinthal, who decided to take matters into his own hands. Buying a generator and making some minor adjustments, Levinthal found that generators not only could run with biodiesel, but that biodiesel cleaned them out and helped keep them in better shape.

From there, Levinthal teamed with partner Chris Wangro and launched GreeNow. Today GreeNow provides generators, forklifts, site lights, and gators all 99-percent powered by biodiesel fuel. They also power their trucks on biodiesel fuel.

Based in lower Manhattan, with a Bronx warehouse, GreeNow has provided green power for the Pope's visit to New York City, as well as the River Festival, Clearwater Music festival, and other events, including those for corporations. They have even provided generators for film shoots and are now working with LEED-certified green builders to use biodiesel at construction sites.

# 16. Chokola'j®
## chokolajchocolate.com

From his days as a chef at four star restaurants and world famous resorts to his new entrepreneurial effort, Chokola'j® Daniel Kennedy always followed his dreams and passions—the Long Island-based home to fine artisan chocolates is no exception. While Daniel creates amazing chocolates in 36 flavors and his wife Susan manages the business end of the company, they are both dedicated to doing their part to help the planet and give back to their community. "We buy ingredients from local farms and farm stands," explains Dan who is a firm believer in natural products, sustainability, and supporting local businesses. "Food is about flavor and making choices based on what is available and what will provide the least impact on the environment while having the best taste," he adds.

Buying cocoa butter from the Rainforest Alliance and using recyclable packaging in everything from the boxes to the paper wrappers, Chokola'j® is truly a scrumptiously green business.

## 17. Selfish Box

### selfishbox.com

What do corporate executives at Microsoft and T-Mobile do for lunch? Well now they have an option of healthy gourmet lunches in recyclable bags from Selfish Box, named as such because it's *"too good to share."* The idea for the lunch catering business came from Thanh Hua, who started the business with her brother-in-law in 2006. "I was looking for something new and so was my brother-in-law, who was a chef," explains Hua. "When I saw how much packaging goes into box lunches, I thought there has to be a better, greener, way," adds Hua, who also focused on the fact that such large companies such as Microsoft and T-Mobile were right nearby in Redmond, Washington.

Today, Selfish Box offers a wide range of gourmet lunches with a variety of ethnic flavors. Packaging is 100 percent biodegradable in bags that are also designed to fit wraps or sandwiches without being wasteful.

Additionally, Hua used her background in technology to create a paperless office with Microsoft tools. Using Microsoft Office, she was able to devise systems of Excel, Word, and other features of the popular office program to do everything from tracking orders to sending invoices via e-mail and even using mobile devices to gauge prices when shopping.

## 18. Sum-Bo-Shine

### sumboshine.com

"Everything starts with a passion, a vision, or a desire, which is basically what I had," says Carolyn Deal, who, following 10 years as a nurse and more than 20 years in the health care field, opened her own organic baby care product business. Passionate about sustainability, healthcare, and children, it was the perfect idea for a grandmother who wanted to launch a business. Working with an FDA-registered lab to formulate and create the actual products, Carolyn built up a line of nine products including baby lotion, diaper ointment, shampoo, and bodywash all made with natural ingredients. Within a year of starting her green business, named for her three children, Summer, Rainbow, and Sunshine (and no, she's not from Southern California) the business has already garnered awards for green products and been written up in *Mothering*, *Wellness*, and other magazines.

Sum-Bo-Shine is not only about healthy, natural products for babies, and new moms, but is also very much aware of packaging. The company not only sells products in recyclable packages, but has a website that allows you to request an envelope in which you can return the empty plastic bottles and they will recycle them for you. Now that's a passion and commitment to the earth all rolled up into one successful new business.

## 19. Electric Body
### electricbody.com

One of several green-minded husband-and-wife teams to launch a business, the Hiestands, Shelly and Denie, came to Los Angeles from New Zealand with an interest in health and body. Together, they formed Electric Body, an all-natural skin care business featuring Electric Body Skin Elixir, an all-in-one face and eye cream, as well as an anti-wrinkle, anti-aging, skin repair treatment.

In the health field for years, Denie became impassioned about not only what people are eating and drinking, but about what they are putting on their skin. "So many people buy recyclable products and organic foods, but are not aware of what they're putting on their skin," says Shelly. "A lot of chemicals are linked to skin cancer, so we've developed a skin care product that we are launching that can take the place of so much of the wasteful, and potentially harmful products that people buy," she adds.

This two-person business was featured in the gift areas at both the Oscar's and the Emmys. In addition, Electric Body already has a popular blog and a large database.

## 20. Montana Stones
### montanastones.com

Why not use some natural resources to start a business? That's exactly what a husband-and-wife team in eastern Montana decided to do. In 2007, Jan and Dean McCabe (no, they are not the Jan & Dean that sung "Surf City") had an idea to use native stones to create cabinet knobs, door knobs, robe knobs, wine bottle stoppers, and other household accessories. Mounted on wood reclaimed from a Montana barn or from a pine forest fire, and simply attached to a brass pedestal, the stones, each unique to itself, provide a touch of nature to your home.

Using all green power, the McCabes have launched their business from their home. Along with their own website, the business is also included on green websites such as ecomall.com and greenpeople.org. The husband-and-wife team are also busily networking with architects, designers, home builders, and others to promote and build their all natural, very unique, business.

# 21. iTySE

## ityse.biz

The answer to the paper or plastic question, according to long time friends Shawna Pierson and Chris Kodama, is a resounding "neither!" Together Piersen and Kodama decided that they would take on a new business venture tapping directly into the green culture by creating iTyse, makers of stylish, eco-friendly, reusable bags for shopping.

"This is a response to the environmental issues with the plastic and paper bags," explains Shawna, adding that people can make the change and bringing their own bags when they go shopping, especially if they are stylish.

The bags, in various colors, are designed to hold plenty of groceries or whatever you are using them for, with each Rib-Stop Nylon bag including four mesh bags within, all manufactured locally. A work program in a local Idaho prison provides inmates with paying jobs and iTySE with employees.

Most significantly, iTySE is at the emergence of what will likely become the new age of reusable bags for shopping. "Seattle has already imposed a $.20 per bag charge and other cities including Portland, Los Angeles, and New York are looking into it. In fact, China has a ban on plastic bags altogether," adds Chris.

In response to doubts from their husbands, Shawna and Chris called the company iTySE, which stands for I Told You So Enterprises.

# 22. Wild Dill

## wilddill.com

Proving once again the power of the internet, Jennifer Doob, a one-person operation, is vying against much larger competitors through her own online business using a well-crafted, professionally designed website that can challenge her larger counterparts.

Selling organic, fair trade, sweatshop-free, natural, and/or recycled clothing and toys for little tykes, Wild Dill lets you be kind to your baby and our planet all at the same time.

The business was launched in February of 2008 from the Bay area. The idea came from a young mom who did not want to go back to work (even though she was working for an environmental nonprofit) and preferred the idea of running a business while spending some quality time at home with her young son Dillon, whom she labeled a bit wild . . . hence the name Wild Dill. "I also wanted a name that had something to do with nature in it, so I looked through some nature books and found dill. Since that was also my son's name it fit perfectly," explains Jennifer.

Scouring boutiques, the internet, and other locations for the most organic products she could find, Jennifer now offers organically made clothing, sleepwear, and play items from more than 40 designers. Many of the manufacturers are locally based, which saves on shipping. Additionally, packaging is recyclable and cornstarch peanuts are used instead of the Styrofoam ones.

▲  ▲  ▲

Each of these 22 businesses has been built with an environmental mindset, and yet the types of businesses differ from brewing beer to selling real estate to selling solar energy to making and selling organic snack foods. The point is that your own particular take on what makes your business green will depend on what you do and how you do it. Visiting the websites of these businesses can give you some ideas that you can hopefully incorporate into your plans for a green business.

# Customers and
## Market Research

Give the people what they want. This is one of the credos you will hear often in business. It makes sense because if you are asking customers to fork over their hard-earned money, they should be buying a product or service that they desire. Therefore, your first question upon starting any type of business is: What do Customers Want? In this case, you are looking for two answers. First, what they want from your product or service and second, what do they want from an environmental perspective, if in fact they know. You need to consider that customers sometimes, but not always, know what they want from a product or service. In the rapidly growing world of green awareness and innovation, there are constantly new discoveries. Remarkably, people in a wide range of industries have taken the time and effort to discover, create, uncover, and/or re-invent natural means of producing any number of items. In keeping up with your industry, you may very likely know what environmentally-minded consumers want before they do.

# What Do Customers Want?

It's a simple question, yet one that has baffled business owners for years. Customers, whether groups, business owners, or individuals, have a wide range of wants and needs that are often hard to bring together under one collective roof. To make matters worse, they are easily swayed by trends, friends, fads, the media, and in many cases the economy or even the government. The multitude of possibilities makes satisfying an expansive customer base a very time-consuming and expensive undertaking, one that most small-business owners cannot afford to tackle. Even Amazon, a giant among e-tailers featuring everything from clothing to household items, started as just an online bookseller. You, too, will likely want to start small as did nearly all of our 22 featured businesses at the end of Chapter 2.

From an environmental perspective customers, by and large, resemble dieters in many ways. They want to be green, or lean, but they still have little willpower when it comes to certain indulgences. They continue to drive to work and leave the air conditioning on all day in the office, while still recycling and supporting environmental causes and concerns. Much like having that salad followed by that must-have piece of cheesecake, it's simply human nature. Customers (most of us, actually) commit to making an effort as long as we are not sacrificing too much of what makes us feel good. Is this wrong? Are we not entitled to our pleasures? You can debate this on your own time. However, from a business perspective, you'll want to find a middle ground that embraces both practicality and the joys of life along with responsibility to the environment. In short, yes, you can indulge a little, just don't throw the packaging material into a landfill, recycle it!

The popular online office supply site, The Green Office.com (thegreenoffice.com), sells green appliances, furnishings, and office supplies along with products that are not at all green. Why you may ask? As founder and CEO Alex Szabo explains, "We want people to be able to do their one-stop office shopping with us so they can find everything they want including the greenest products, light green products, and conventional alternatives."

As Szabo sees it, at least this way they will include some green products while waiting for other product areas to catch up. By letting it be known that customers are looking for greener products in certain areas, companies like Szabo's can also influence manufacturers in the non-green areas to seek out greener alternatives.

While surveys routinely show that customers would opt for green alternatives in many areas, there are still some product areas that have not yet become satisfactory to the green buying market. Once upon a time many health food stores suffered because buyers just did not like the alternatives sold as "healthier" versions of traditional fare. Today, however, food makers have come a long way and organic and "health" foods are much better received than they were a decade ago. Customers are still discerning, but while they are looking for quality, they are also looking for eco-friendly products and packaging. Little by little industries are embracing green, as it pertains to both sustainability and practicality.

The other factor that needs to be considered is that fewer than 20 percent of the consumer population is particularly immersed in "green." This group—the dark green environmentalists—are knowledgeable about the environment and work sustainability into their lifestyles whenever possible. The problem, however, is that the other 80-plus percent of the population are not really part of a "green" demographic. They can, and typically do, learn about green products and services, based on what they need and what affects them personally, rather than learning about environmentalism in broader terms.

"Most people won't proceed head first into things such as sustainability and the environment. Instead, they have one or two things that pertain to them that they will want to find more information about," explains David Anderson, founder and publisher of Greenoptions.com. The website was originally launched as a site focusing on the environment from a broad perspective but in the fall of 2007 switched to a format featuring several sites with blogs and information on various eco-topics, such as a green building site, transportation/bio fuel site, a family site, and so on. "The reason we broke it into topics on separate sites is because green options and green portals are popping up all over the place and people tend to get overwhelmed. This way someone could look at the cars site and find information of interest to them, while also learning about green options," explains Anderson, adding that the Eco-Child's Play site is one of the most popular. "One major driver that makes people start thinking about going green is if they have a baby. They want to start thinking about bringing nontoxic items into their home, like cleaning supplies. They start focusing on parenting issues as it applies to them and then start learning about green alternatives. Then you can start to expose them to things like organic foods or energy efficiency in their homes and so on," adds Anderson, further explaining the idea of finding a common denominator with potential customers.

As is the case with most businesses, people will have initial interest because what you are offering pertains to their specific needs. So, as Anderson and others recommend, meet them at their point of interest and then introduce some green into their world.

# Exploring Your Target Market

Nothing will appeal to "everyone," so you will need to zero in on your target audience. In other words, who will buy your products or services? The concept for targeting customers with a green product is not particularly different than targeting any other customers. You need, first and foremost, to have a quality product or service that solves their problem and meets their needs. You also need to do plenty of research, both primary and secondary, to create a portrait of who it is that will be buying your product or services. Questions regarding your target market help you identify:

- Gender
- Age range
- Marital status
- Highest level of education completed
- Annual household income range
- Approximate annual amount of money spent in your industry
- Possibly, how much more they will spend for a greener version of that product

> **Beware!**
> Curb assumptions. One of the most common but often most misleading means of utilizing marketing data is to make generalizations or assumptions about a group based on a few answers to a questionnaire or survey. Make sure you have a lot of pieces of the puzzle before you determine what your demographic group wants and needs. Don't bring in pre-conceived ideas or biases either.

Again, remember that not everyone is knowledgeable about green benefits, so you may need to build slowly, meeting various needs, in some cases, with traditional products. While you can certainly build green awareness with new products and strategies, it is often advantageous to include a range of possibilities, some of which may not yet be green. This is what Greenoffice.com has done successfully.

While you can approach your potential customers by the more traditional means of determining what it is they are looking for in a product and service, and then introduce green options, you can also see if your audience does have some green interests or concerns. For example, you might create a questionnaire that inquires as to which of the following are the most important environmental concerns to them personally. This will typically tie into their personal life situation.

- Renewable energy
- Transportation and fuel
- Indoor air quality and home environment
- Organic foods and healthy eating
- Planting, gardening, and/or agriculture

These are just some examples. Respondents can be asked to check off one or more areas that they feel most strongly about. Your goal is to find out where you can best make a dent since it's very difficult (and potentially time consuming) to try appeasing everyone at once.

Within any, or several of the sectors listed above, you can actively work to establish your business model by creating innovative technologies and making and/or selling products on which your business can grow and thrive. You can also work to promote the transformation to new methodology as an alternative to using conventional sectors. For example, if you are finding that many of your target audience are concerned about high energy costs, then you can promote renewable energy sources rather than conventional energy sources, much as the California-based company Solar Wind Works does (mentioned in the previous chapter).

You will also find a completely separate market of individuals not yet oriented to environmental causes and concerns, and this is a large group, which is hard to define. Therefore, you need to first define a target group within your industry, such as consumers for sportswear in the 16- to 25-year-old age range. Then you can start thinking about how much of this market is eco-savvy.

Doing market research can take some time and typically cost you a few dollars. In the end, however, knowing who your market is, for any type of product or service, is essential to your success. Your best means of researching the market is a combination of reviewing data from reliable sources, which might include:

- Websites
- The local planning board
- Government sources including the census numbers

## Dollar Stretcher

While in the throes of setting up a business, it can be hard to spend a great deal of time doing research. This is where research assistants come in handy. What better place to find cost-effective assistants than at local colleges and even high schools. If you can meet with the heads of the internship program and show them your business plan and impress upon them that you are starting up a new green business, you may be able to utilize the ability of enthusiastic, eco-minded interns to help you do the research to find your target audience.

- A good business library
- Conversations with residents and business owners.
- Local associations, community groups, and certainly any green organizations located in your area (or areas) of business
- The media, including back copies of articles

# Focus Groups

Focus groups are a great way to find out what your potential future customers are thinking. Contrary to popular belief, focus groups are rather inexpensive to run. A good focus group features a facilitator who is likeable (but not pushy or aggressive) and well-versed in running such a group. This means that he or she knows how to keep everyone included in the discussion and steer the proceedings in such a manner that they stay on the topic.

In addition, a good focus group should also:

- Have a rough budget.
- Be held in a quiet, comfortable, well-lit, easily accessible location for everyone involved (reserve the site in advance).
- Have a clear and defined purpose. Gathering general opinions is not as effective as finding out what people think about specific areas of interest, products, services, your promotional or advertising campaign, etc.
- Consist of a defined group of people. This way you are getting answers from the segment of the population you want to reach. (Contact people with a couple of weeks notice if possible.)
- Consist of a manageable size, such as 12 to 25 people. Larger groups can be more difficult from a management and size perspective.
- Follow a roughly scripted outline so that all areas of significance are covered in the allotted time.
- Run less than two hours and include a break of about 20 minutes.
- Include at least snacks, or beverages, if not a full lunch (depending on your budget).
- Provide all necessary materials (gather all of this—and run copies if necessary—in advance)
- Have a means of recording the session and using such information for post-focus-group follow up and analysis.
- Include thanking participants and even providing a small reward or incentive for having taken part. Be careful that this is small enough not to attract

unwanted people simply for the reward, but large enough to make people feel that they can spare two hours of their time (plus travel time). This could be, for example, $50 per participant.

Naturally, your focus group can include green topics, but unless you are going to market only to a "darker" green audience, keep it open to all levels of green—even those who have not yet discovered green. The key is to zero in on what you want to know from the participants regarding their needs and your products and introduce green examples in conjunction with your business. In some instances, you will find a market already prepared and waiting. Don't forget, in any niche group you will find people who are well-versed on the types of products and/or services your business offers. In some cases they already want greener versions of traditional products, while in other cases, you will be forging new ground. Again, determine in advance what types of questions you want to ask and then look for answers that can benefit your business. Also, try to gauge the knowledge and interest in the environment of the specific group. Some businesses will cater to a green-ready group, while many businesses will have to introduce greener alternatives.

The biggest flaws in focus groups are:

- Not assembling the right group of people.
- Not asking the right questions. This results in not obtaining the information that you want/need for your business.
- Having a moderator that does not bring out the best in people. Moderators can be self involved or simply not likeable, both of which can kill the enthusiasm.
- Not using the research obtained for your benefit. Why have a focus group if you aren't going to benefit from it?

The bottom line is that focus groups can be very helpful, but the preliminary and follow-up work is just as, if not more, important than the actual time spent in the focus group itself.

# Utilizing Your Research

From your research, you can usually find four groups of potential customers. There are those that are:

1. ready to buy now.
2. ready to buy under certain conditions.
3. need convincing to buy.
4. not interested at all.

Using your research, you can figure out how to get that first group of immediate buyers into your business today. You then need to know what conditions will draw the second group and have a campaign to educate and lure the third group. Group four is not usually worth your time and marketing expenses, at least not until you have built up enough business from the other three groups.

Fortunately today, a lot of eco-friendly products and services are crossing over to the mainstream market. Even without knowing it, consumers are buying more organic hair care and cleaning products. There are many more recyclable products hitting the mainstream shelves and, from a service perspective, providers are often thinking in greener terms regarding how they do business, particularly as builders, architects, designers, and landscapers. Businesses are also creating greener environments in which consumers shop even without necessarily being aware of the eco-factors involved. For example, Wal-Mart's drive to buy from greener suppliers isn't always obvious to the consumer, yet it is part of their effort to benefit the environment.

# Niche Markets

Within nearly every industry you will find niche markets. Under the "green" umbrella, you may or may not find yours. RideSpring, for example, has zeroed in on the alternative transportation/green commuting market by establishing company websites accessible by members of a given office to help arrange carpools. The site also encourages all forms of alternative transportation by providing incentive prizes for steady green commuters. The point is that the business is focused on a market within the green community . . . alternative, energy-saving commuting.

Essentially, there are two types of green business models.

First, there are those with specific green solutions such as RideSpring, Solar Wind Works, or a company selling hybrid vehicles or organic foods. They are operating a business that sells green products or services.

The other type is a more mainstream business, like Wal-Mart or Starbucks, that utilizes green methodology, processes, and practices in running the business but does not rely on drawing a specific green-oriented market. While some of the products and services will be green, that is not the emphasis of the business. These businesses draw from a larger target audience. Of course, the choice will be yours based on how big a business you are starting as well as your industry, products (or services), and location.

Typically, the way in which a business reaches out to its target audience is by finding a means of connecting with the buying market. For example, if you are selling baby care products, find out the best ways and means of reaching out to, and appealing to, new parents in your area, especially new moms, and let them know more about what you offer. First draw them in based on their needs as parents and their possible environmental concerns. As David Anderson mentioned earlier, "People tend to start thinking greener when it affects them personally." Therefore, someone car hunting will be more interested in hybrid vehicles than someone who is neither in the market for a car nor a car enthusiast. If, for example, your new business is in the building industry, your clients will come to you with their needs, some of which may be green and others only green enough to meet federal and local standards. First you want to appeal to them as builders who can complete the job in a professional manner, within their

> **Tip...**
>
> **Smart Tip**
>
> In most surveys taken in the past five years, more than 75 percent of customers say they will pay a little bit more for a greener product if they feel it meets their needs. With that statistic in mind, you need to first impress upon customers that your product meets their needs, then note that it is environmentally friendlier or organic.

budgetary constraints (if possible) then you want to respond to their green needs or introduce them to some greener building alternatives. Hint: If you can save your clients money in the long run, it will be of particular interest.

In short, you can certainly build a green niche within your broader market. In some areas, such as organic products, you can venture more easily into a niche than in others, since many of the products have gone mainstream. "You can look at anything through a green lens," says David Anderson. The question is how green? You want to build a target audience from a larger population, or the 80+ percent who have not yet become dark green or are not yet as environmentally informed, while having some appeal to that 15 to 20 percent who are already there.

# Scouting the Competition

Any good entrepreneur will want to, or actually need to, know what the competition is up to. This means finding out exactly what competing businesses in your industry are doing. Direct competition are those businesses in your immediate area, while indirect competition may come from other businesses that happen to sell some of the products, or offer some of the services, that you offer. For example, a new car-wash owner will scout competitors in a reasonable geographic area as his or her direct competition. Filling stations that also wash cars might be considered indirect competition.

So, what is it you want to know about your competitors? Here are a few things to consider:

- What are their prices?

- Where does their pricing fit within the industry? Bargain? High end? Somewhere in between?
- What kind of special deals (or sales) do they offer?
- What type of promotion and marketing do they do?
- What type of customers do they attract? Students? Yuppies? Forty somethings? Seniors?
- How up to date are they? Making or selling the latest models? Selling yesterday's models?
- What type of customer service do they provide?
- How attentive are they to customer questions and concerns? (Play the role of an inquiring customer and find out.)
- What do you feel are their strong points?
- Where could they be doing a better job?
- Are they green? Are they greenwashing? Somewhere in between?

The more you study what your competition is and is not doing, the more carefully you can craft your business to offer customers some alternatives. If you can provide options that they are not providing—whether it means additional product choices, a larger menu of services, better customer service, or greater attention to customers needs—the more likely you will set yourself apart from your competitors.

Another avenue of competition that you will need to explore is the internet. Almost every business has a presence on the internet, even if you are not selling or marketing your products or services directly through a site. Therefore, you'll want to see what sites your competitors have and be at least as clever in establishing your web presence. If you are in sales, you should look at websites that are your indirect competition and then offer customers something they cannot get by making a purchase online, which is typically personalized attention and the opportunity to see, feel, try on, or check out a product firsthand.

If, however, your business is primarily an online business, or you anticipate a good percentage of your business coming from online customers, then you need to scour the competitive websites very carefully. Your site needs to be easier to navigate, offer more content, provide more accessibility to products and/or services, or simply have a better layout. The key is to find a way to keep customers coming back to your site by giving them incentives, content to read, interactive options, and so forth—more on building a good website later.

In short, market research dictates that you determine how many competitors you are up against, what they offer, and what they charge customers. The two big questions you need to answer honestly are:

1. Will there be a large enough slice of the pie for your business in your geographic area, on the internet (if you are an e-tailer), or in the overall industry?
2. Can you find a competitive edge?

Scouting the competition is the only way to determine whether you have a realistic chance of gaining a market share.

Many business owners with a real desire to make a difference are able to pass that passion on to customers, and that is a strong selling point. However, as more green-minded entrepreneurs plant their seeds as business owners, you will need to do more from a business perspective, which may mean better customer service or greener customer service. Do what your competitors are not yet doing. If they are still offering paper or plastic, then you should be offering canvas reusable bags, not just as a competitive edge, but because it's better for the environment. Again, leading with your beliefs can pay off.

Of course scouting the competition before you open is only half the battle. You need to stay abreast of what your competitors are doing on a regular basis. Keep an eye on their product lines, services offered, expansion, pricing policies, and green activities. You want to continue to draw new customers while maintaining your current ones.

# The 80–20 Rule

Remember that in most businesses 80 percent of your business will come from regular customers while 20 percent will come from new business. Too many business owners spend an inordinate amount of time chasing new business, while neglecting to maintain their steady customers. Since it typically costs significantly more money to chase new customers than maintain regular ones, this is not at all cost effective.

Being on the edge of everything that is green can benefit you in that you're connecting with your customers on something that is important to both you as a business owner and them as new parents, new car buyers, new home buyers, or wherever their interests lie . . . and have a green side to them.

We'll talk more about the objectives of maintaining steady customers while also going after new ones later in the book. Of course to start out, you have no choice but to seek out new customers. By doing your marketing research, knowing about your target audience, and being ready with solutions to their problems, you can help build a customer base of people who will become your regulars and stay with you for a long time.

# Common Market Research Errors

Finally, when planning and proceeding through the course of your market research, it's a good idea to review some of the mistakes commonly made by others so you'll know what not to do.

Consider the following errors:

1. *Taking too broad an approach.* Before embarking on your research, you need to set up some objectives. You know your product(s) and should have an idea of your potential customers. Therefore, you should not be seeking any type of customer, but focusing on a specific target audience, or niche. Too often, in an attempt to find customers, any customers, business owners go out marketing without knowing what they are looking for and end up with useless data.

2. *Utilizing too many junk responses.* You need to have some control over where your surveys or questionnaires go and who answers them. Likewise, you need the right people at your focus group. If nothing else, you need to weed out junk responses, or those filled out by people who are not at all in your potential buying audience or by people (often kids) just having fun or looking for an incentive, such as winning a prize. Find out the best way to reach the right group of people rather than just getting "any" responses. Junk responses can be misleading and ultimately useless.

3. *Making it too difficult for responders.* If the questions are complicated or the survey takes too long to answer, you'll limit yourself. Many business owners, in an effort to get too much information, ask too much, expect too much. and delve into people's personal data, losing the respondents. Make your market research simple and to the point.

4. *Not utilizing the data properly or at all.* Good data follow up means taking your market research data and breaking it down into groups and categories that can help you target your best customers. Determine what statistics will best serve your purpose and pull them from your research. Too often, business owners pull only the numbers they are looking for and do not get a realistic picture from their market research efforts. Either that, or they do nothing with the responses, which makes the efforts a complete waste of time.

Keep these common mistakes in mind. Do the necessary planning before and the data review and statistical summaries after you conduct your market research for the best results.

# Building Your Green Business

## Names, Structures, Locations, and Energy Options

Naming a business is a fun, yet thought-provoking process. You want a name that defines what your business does, while being easy to say and quite memorable all at the same time. If you intend to make a green statement in all that you do, you may want to work the environmental angle into your name. Eco-minded companies such as Clif Bar or New

Belgium Brewery did not incorporate green into their names but into all that they do, and it did not work against them by any means. However, other businesses have gone with the green angle, using "organic," "eco," "environment," or the word "green" in their names. Kelly LaPlante Organic Interior Designs offers the name of the designer, giving it a personal touch, the word "organic" providing the green touch, and "designs," so you know what the business is all about.

Then these are other green businesses such as Earth Friendly Goods, which sells a wide range of environmentally-friendly products made from hemp, bamboo, organic cottons, etc. Green Apple Kitchen, which is a more niche-oriented business featuring earth-friendly kitchen tools and accessories. While looking at "green" business names, you'll also find:

- Natural4Less
- Green Spirit Store
- EcoSource
- My Green Home
- Enviroshop
- Ecobooks
- Eco Gift Wrap
- Parenting by Nature
- Atlantis Natural
- Mother Earth Nursery Design
- EcoBaby
- Greenfeet
- Organics 4 Your Pets
- Our Happy Hound's Organic Biscuit Bakery
- Natural High Lifestyle
- Earth Speaks Organic
- Wearable Vegetables
- EcoUnique
- Natural Tree Furniture
- BaliBamboo Creations
- EcoDesignz
- Sustainable Paper Supplies
- The Green Office
- GoGreen Labels
- It's Only Natural Gifts

These are just a few of the numerous green, environmental business names. Of course some are more defining than others: It's Only Natural Gifts, Natural Tree Furniture, or the Green Office let you know that they are green and what they sell; some, such as Greenfeet, would have you believe they might sell footwear, which isn't the case.

You will want to provide potential customers with a feel for your business, while being green is a plus. However, don't limit yourself with a word that may box you in. For example, if you are Mickey's Recyclable Lamps, you may also want to sell other types of recycled furniture, or furniture made from environmentally friendly materials. Therefore you might opt for Mickey's Eco-Lamps and Furniture. As you can see from the list above, you can make it simple, sell green, and also let people know the types of products you offer.

When thinking about your business name, also consider your domain name since nearly every business today has a web presence. You will want to look up names and register a domain name with a company. More on this momentarily.

# Making Your Business Name Official

Whether you are doing business locally or internationally, you still need to be a registered business somewhere—the IRS likes to know where to find you. For this reason you will need to register your business locally. Make sure you do a business name search before registering. You do this for three reasons:

1. It ensures that no one else in your local area is using the name and gives you dibs on it, so to speak.
2. It makes your local authorities happy. Most cities or counties require that you have a fictitious business name or dba (doing business as). This way, they can keep tabs on you for tax or other licensing purposes, and you go on public record so anyone who wants or needs to can look up the name of your company and find the name of the owner.
3. Most banks won't allow you to open a business checking account—one with your company name, which gives you credibility among suppliers and others—unless you can show them proof that you have registered a fictitious business name.

Obtaining a dba is quick and easy, and you can absolutely do it on your own. The process varies a bit in different states and regions of the country, but the local licensing bureau will fill you in on what you need—call them to get the details, or go to their website, before making the trip to the licensing bureau.

For your website, make sure the domain name you want is available. It should be as similar to your business name as possible and end in .com, or perhaps .net. Don't let anyone sell you on other suffixes. Despite the fact that it can sometimes be difficult to get the .com name you want, .com still rules the business world.

Of course you will need to do a domain name search prior to registering a domain name. One way to do this is by going to networksolutions.com and checking to see if your name choices are available. Following the easy directions, check to see if the domain name you've chosen has already been taken. If it has, choose another. When you find a permutation that is available, register it online.

## Smart Tip

## Tip...

Since so many domains are already being used, you should think up several versions of the name you want in case one or more have already been taken. Businesses will often buy the closest misspellings to their own name, or similar variations.

Of course when thinking of a name, it not only has to look and sound right, but also it needs to be easy to spell and remember. Use the Business Naming Worksheet on the next page. Also, for the sake of typing in a web address, don't make it too long. Nobody wants to type Janandfredsgoodoldfashionedorganicicecream.com. Perhaps, Jan and Fred could opt for organicicecream.com or if that's taken J&Forganicice cream.com. Play with the possibilities but keep it simple enough so that bad typists— and that's most of us—don't have to re-enter it five or six times. Along with paying for a domain name, you can also register a name, or even a logo or slogan (if no one else uses it) as a trademark—which takes some time. You can find out information and do a trademark search through the U.S. Trademark and Patent Office at uspto.gov. You can also hire an attorney or a trademark search firm to handle the job for you (for a fee, of course).

# Business Structures

Green business or otherwise, you will need to determine your business structure. Most commonly, small businesses are sole proprietorships, which are, by all accounts, the easiest structures under which to run a business. You get a business license and file the necessary business forms applicable within your state and *voila!*, you are in business. There is very little paperwork and few formalities, other than paying taxes. Your income is reported on your personal or jointly filed tax return. The drawback, however, is that if your business gets sued, so do you—personally. In other words, you are held liable and it can put a serious dent in your personal finances. In a litigious society, you may feel more comfortable taking greater precautions.

# Business Naming Worksheet

List five environmental words you might want to use in your name

1. _____

2. _____

3. _____

4. _____

5. _____

List five words or groups of two or three words that sum up what your business does

1. _____

2. _____

3. _____

4. _____

5. _____

List five combinations of the above words

1. _____

2. _____

3. _____

4. _____

5. _____

## Business Naming Worksheet, continued

Add other word(s) to make your title unique. This could include your area, if your business has a local following, such as "East Greenville's Eco-Furnishings" or your name or names "Jim & Stacy's Organically Baked Tasties."

1. _____

2. _____

3. _____

4. _____

5. _____

Incorporating is another option for entrepreneurs. When you're incorporated, the corporation carries the liability instead of you personally. You can also use such incorporation more effectively when negotiating with banks. Even though the bank will probably still ask you for a personal guarantee, you can use your corporate status during such negotiations.

The biggest plus for incorporating is that the business stands as a separate entity—meaning that you are typically not personally held liable if your product or service injures someone or you are sued for some other business-related reason. However, with incorporation comes a lot of paperwork and various requirements that you must fulfill as set forth by the state in which you incorporate. One drawback of incorporating may mean double taxation. In this case, you pay taxes as a corporation and then again on the money that you personally take out as your salary. Your business attorney and accountant will advise you on how to handle such matters.

Another, somewhat newer, possibility is forming a Limited Liability Corporation (LLC), which is something of a hybrid between incorporating and going solo. The advantages of forming an LLC are that the owner, or owners, are afforded limited liability and have pass-through taxes similar to a partnership. By forming an LLC, rather than a corporation, you receive nearly all of the benefits of a corporation but avoid some of the drawbacks, such as double taxation, some requirements, and excessive paperwork. Again, discuss this with a business attorney and/or your accountant to determine if this would work for you.

Partnerships can be trickier than one would imagine. There are many areas that need to be addressed when forming a partnership and they should all be spelled out in a detailed partnership agreement. You will also need to determine in advance whether one of you is a silent partner or a limited partner. Discuss ahead of time what each partner's responsibilities are and only go into a partnership with someone you truly believe you can get along with on a day-to-day basis. Even then, many well-meaning partners have ended up with major disagreements, ending friendships and straining family relationships.

**Beware!**
Partnership agreements should always include an out clause. This is a means of allowing one partner or the other end their participation as a partner. By establishing this in advance, you can make it clear how you can break up the partnership without ending up fighting in a court battle.

# Zoning Regulations

Zoning regulations are established to separate business and residential areas (or zones) from one another. This is primarily to limit commercial traffic as well as parking and garbage pick up from quieter residential neighborhoods. It is also used to separate various types of businesses based on their needs. For example, businesses that require more room for parking or have a greater flow of traffic may be in an area that is separated from smaller mom and pop shops. There are various other reasons for zoning laws and some such laws divide up different types of businesses. For example, some areas are reserved for non-chain stores, while others may not have drive-thrus. In some cases, a certain type of business, such as a rowdy bar, may not be allowed to open within x blocks from a school. Your main objective, however, is to determine the zoning laws in the area(s) that you wish to open a business.

From a green perspective, you may need to know if an area is zoned for setting up wind turbines or if you can grow your own foods. Whatever your goals, you will also need to find out if they fit into the zoning ordinances of the area in which you'd like to set up shop. If you plan to operate a business from your home, you also need to look at the zoning regulations. Signage is a major factor that often comes into play for home business owners. Find out what you can and cannot do ahead of time.

# Finding a Green Location

Not only can you start a green business, you can find a green location in which to set up shop. This may be a green office building, green office park, or even a strip mall. Factors that make a location green include:

- The building materials used in the structure. Are they environmentally friendly?
- Indoor materials. Are these also eco-friendly, such as nontoxic, non-lead paints, bamboo, natural-fiber carpets, etc.?
- The type of energy used in the building. Is it renewable?
- The type of equipment in the building. Is it Energy Star and eco-friendly?
- The grounds on which the building sits. Are there green areas or is everything asphalt? Was it built over a landfill?
- The use of water. Is rainwater collected and used? Is water reused where possible? Are chemicals kept out of the water?
- Is the building maintained in an environmentally friendly manner?
- Is there waste management and recycling?

## World's Greenest Building

**W**hile there will certainly be some debate, there are many people in the Maryland, Delaware, Virginia area who consider The Phillip Merrill Environmental Center owned by the Chesapeake Bay Foundation to be the world's "greenest" building.

The building is made entirely of either recycled materials or materials that were created in such a manner not to be detrimental to the environment. For clean, fresh air, there is a controllable ventilation system along with a rainwater system designed to capture the water so it can be used for cleaning. Within the building, you'll find natural lighting in many areas and environmental interior flooring made from cork, bamboo, and what is called "natural linoleum." While there are a number of buildings in other towns and cities now being built with similar green qualities, this is one of the most prestigious eco-buildings in full operation today.

- The HVAC system. How old is it? Is it routinely maintained? Are there separate zone control thermostats?
- Is the building up to date on asbestos removal, lead paint exposure, and have all unsafe materials been removed?

Many newly constructed buildings, and most of those being restored, refurbished, or renovated are becoming greener, not just because of the need to meet environmental standards, but in order to attract eco-minded tenants such as yourself. In fact, the United States Green Building Council (USGBC) rates, and gives awards to, the greenest buildings they can find, some of which may have space for your business. The USGBC Certification program, known as Leadership in Energy and Environmental Design, or LEED, was first established in 2000, and has since awarded certification to 715 buildings throughout the United States. With contractors and architects becoming more conscious of the demand for greener surroundings, there will certainly be more eco-friendly buildings on the way. However, since there are no single standards, you will need to make the judgment regarding whether the office, store, factory space, or other location meets the needs of your business and is an eco-friendly environment.

The other question to ask when leasing space is what changes you can and cannot make to the facility. This will vary greatly depending on the landlord or ownership group. Can you bring in a more energy efficient HVAC system? Can you install a skylight so you won't need to work that HVAC system to such a great extent?

Of course, buying a property will give you far more latitude when it comes to greening it. On the other hand, before you buy, as a business owner you'll want to look closely at the real estate market. Ask yourself:

- What are the trends in real estate in the region in which I am looking to open a business?
- What is the potential for growth in terms of the surrounding area?
- Are there reasons to think the area is on an economic upswing? Downswing?
- Can you expand on the property, literally?

While leasing means you can pick up and move if your business is struggling because of the location, buying makes it that much tougher. Of course it will depend on the type of business and your goals and needs. No, you won't be able to grow a major corporation with 300 employees from a small rented facility, but you may not be planning or looking for that size business.

For some businesses, such as stores and many service businesses location is a major factor; others, such as e-business or those that depend on shipping their products elsewhere, can be run from virtually anywhere (no pun intended).

# Know Your Business Needs

For a retail store, you need a high-traffic location, parking, easy access to main roads, room for shipping and storage. You need to distance yourself from too much competition and be able to turn a profit on top of what is often a high-rent proposition.

Requirements for a factory or manufacturing business will differ depending on the type of product. Some products are made in a home environment while others need significant space. Location is important only as it pertains to being accessible for transport, shipping, resources, and the necessary space in and around the facility.

Service businesses typically need smaller spaces and may do fine without a prime location from a visibility standpoint, but still must be easily accessible if clients, students, or customers are coming to you.

Office-based businesses often have more choices with buildings and office parks available. Here, too, it will depend on your type of business as to whether you will need a primary location. If clients, distributors, or vendors will be coming by for frequent visits then you may want a more accessible area. If, however, you are running a web business or mail order business, your office can be on the outskirts of town, as long as it's accessible to you.

Accessibility is something you will want to consider carefully when starting a green business. "Nobody whom we work with is more than three miles away," says Folake Kuye, founder and owner of WeWe Clothing, the homebased business in Beverly Hills, California, that sells mostly organic clothing for young children. They use a variety of people to cut, sew, and create the clothes that Kuye designs, all of whom are right nearby. "I bike to places I need to go, or even use my skateboard," she adds. The same is true for another California business, Kelly LaPlante Organic Design, Inc., where most people bike or walk to the office.

Companies today are looking more closely at their shipping and transportation needs when deciding upon a location. Clif Bar went so far as to relocate their Southern California distribution sites to be closer to their sales locations. They also shifted to fuel efficient vehicles and biodiesel.

Ask yourself:

- Can employees, vendors, and distributors get to and from my primary location(s) in environmentally friendly manners if they so choose?
- Do customers need to make a special trip by car to our location or are we near mass transit, accessible by bike, or in an area in which they can cover most of their shopping needs?
- Do we have nearby sources for products and goods? For example, if you are in the business of selling food (as either a store of a restaurant) can you get fresh produce locally?

- Are you near a recycling center? There are many to be found. See if you have some in your area.

# Building Green from the Ground Up

**Smart Tip**

Natural Light: Does the location get natural lighting? You can minimize the HVAC needs with sunroofs and/or large windows to let in sunlight. Look at natural light as a potential money saver on energy bills.

If you can afford to buy the land and build, then you can make an effort to lay a green foundation, so to speak. Buildings of all sizes are being constructed today that utilize environmental architecture in part of, or throughout, a facility. Most green building today is achieved through an integrated process that begins during the pre-design phase. New structures are typically seen as whole buildings from the start, since the systems and components are integrated. This type of preparation is called "whole building design," meaning that the structures are created so that the entire building acts as one fluent system. Within the plan can be the use of renewable energy, environmentally sound means of waste disposal, and the use of rain water, which can even be incorporated into the water needs of the building,

The goals of green building include:

- Using sustainable, earth-friendly building materials. You'll want nontoxic materials with minimal if any chemical emissions, known as low in Volatile Organic Compounds (VOC). You will also want materials that do not require toxic or VOC-producing chemicals for their assembly.

- Energy efficiency, which means minimizing "traditional" energy use while providing the same benefits and comforts.

- Water efficiency, which can employ various ways to limit wasting water, while finding ways of reusing it.

- Excellent indoor air quality. This is a broad term that can include anything from nontoxic paints and chemicals to eco-friendly flooring as well as good ventilation.

- Utilizing the land in an efficient manner, which can include anything from landscaping to bicycle paths to environmentally friendly non-asphalt parking lots (grass).

- Utilizing local materials and resources when building to cut down on shipping, which also means saving significant energy.

Renewable, recyclable, and environmentally responsible materials are what you are seeking when planning to build green. There are numerous green-minded architects who are knowledgeable and experienced in sustainable building who will advise you regarding the best materials and walk you through a life-cycle assessment. Of course this will depend, in part, on the size and scope of your needs and where you are located. Along with recycled materials, you will also find that there are certified woods and various organic products that can be used in the building process. Many green builders are also good at finding and utilizing local reusable materials, such as wood salvaged from old barns, which is becoming more widely used in some areas of the country.

The U.S. Green Building Council (USGBC) is one place to find out more about LEED, a Green Building Rating System®. You'll find them at usgbc.org.

You may also visit the American Institute of Architects at aia.org or the Sustainable Building sourcebook at greenbuilder.com/sourcebook.

> ## Smart Tip Tip...
> Architects and builders will detail each "green" aspect of the project from the ground up. Such details are in the standard building specifications, or "specs." Make sure that you are working with a green architect and that the specs include the green ideas that you discuss ahead of time. In short, review the specs and make sure all of the green ideas and plans are worked into the building contract in advance.

# Leasing Versus Buying and Building

Again, this is a question that faces new entrepreneurs, who can also toss in the third option of starting out at home. Leasing space is a marvelous means of getting your feet wet and your business established in an area. It is a way to test the waters and determine if this is a place in which you can grow, while establishing a customer base.

In some cases you will outgrow your location, meaning that when the lease is up you can look for a larger space. In other cases, the space may be more than you need, in which case you should find out before signing the lease as to whether you can sublet some of the space to another new, growing business.

Leasing is obviously less costly than buying an existing structure. However, you need to sit down with an attorney and go over the terms of the lease very carefully, especially if you are thinking that the location needs some greening. You'll need to find out specifically what you can and cannot do in the leased space. In addition, you'll need to know how much the rent can be raised at the end of the lease. Too many lessees are forced to move when their leases end because the rents are hiked too high.

Owning an existing building gives you much greater leeway to do as you wish, which can allow your green spirit to thrive. However, to buy a property, you need to have it checked out very carefully to make sure it meets your needs and that you won't have to overhaul the facility. Buying a facility and having to make significant changes, especially to make it sustainable, may be more costly than your new business can withstand. Buying means you must be certain that you want this to be your business home for some time. This also means doing some investigation to see what is being planned in and around the location in the future. Will real estate values plummet? Will changes to the landscape cause you to lose business? Careful due diligence is highly recommended.

If you plan to buy land and then build, you have even greater potential to start off on the green foot. However, you will need that much more money to afford land and building costs. You'll also need to know the local ordinances and what you are and are not allowed to do with the land; not every area is wind-turbine friendly for example. Building your own facility will generally allow you the most flexibility in terms of the overall design of your business, as well as your environmental concerns. However, it is much more costly, and a major risk for a new business owner. It also takes much more time until you can open your doors for business.

The home business is a growing reality of our culture, thanks in large part to technology and the means in which it is easy to communicate. A small home business can flourish without much overhead. And if you can maintain a green lifestyle, your carbon footprint can be very minimal. Several of the companies featured in our 22 green business examples in Chapter Two are run from a home base. Many major businesses, such as Lillian Vernon, started at home. In fact, she began her catalog empire from her kitchen table. Homebased businesses are growing at a significant rate and serving as green from the start in part because of the lack of commuting.

# Finding a Green Builder, Architect, and/or Contractor

Today, more and more builders, architects, and contractors focus on sustainability in design and construction. If you are building or even renovating a space, you can now get expert advice on going green (and find numerous architects) from The American Institute of Architects, aia.org. You'll also want to take a look at The United State's Green Business Council's website at usgbc.org. The USGBC is a nonprofit community of leaders who work together to help make green buildings available to everyone. They provide plenty of information including workshops, courses, and LEED reference guides. As defined by the USGBC, in regards to your business environment, LEED certification provides independent, third-party verification that a building project is environmentally responsible, profitable, and a healthy place to work.

Prior to bringing in an architect or contractor to build, rebuild, or renovate your business locale, you will want to learn a little about green architecture, including building materials, sustainability, water efficiency, energy needs, and indoor air quality.

As is typically the case with hiring a professional, you will want to look at credentials, review some previous jobs, and perhaps check out some green references. See if the architect, contractor, or builder has a portfolio of some previous projects and if he or she belongs to any green organizations. If you have specific areas of concern for your business, you'll want to ask about the architect's experience in those areas. In addition, you will want to find out how a contractor or builder works. You are looking for someone who does not contaminate the environment while in the building process and even recycles and reuses older materials.

Your job is to tell a true green architect, contractor, or builder from one who has simply jumped on the green bandwagon and is doing some "greenwashing."

Reaching 100 percent sustainability may be a tall order, but if you are building from the ground up, you can aim to be as green as possible.

# Brownfields

One option for a green location is a Brownfield. This term refers to a location that is typically an abandoned building, such as an old factory, warehouse, or gas station. It can also refer to vacant land. The U.S. EPA defines a Brownfield as" *Real property, the expansion, redevelopment, or reuse of which may be complicated by the presence or potential presence of a hazardous substance, pollutant, or contaminant.*

Brownfields can be the result of a poor economy or a company needing to move to a newer, more prosperous location. Whatever the reason, such a location can be much cheaper than building from scratch or buying a new facility. The two caveats are:

1. Can you find the owners of the property? This sometimes takes some searching.
2. How much will it cost to fix up the facility and bring it up to code? Often, these buildings are far from green and need a lot of work. This may or may not make such a move cost effective. You will need engineers and Brownfield Development specialists to evaluate the property and let you know what needs to be done.

In contrast to new building—which can be a leading cause of carbon emissions leading to pollution—redevelopment of a Brownfield can be a productive manner of utilizing existing land. It's a significant definition of the word "reuse," which plays a major part in going green. In the course of eliminating what is often an unsafe, potentially hazardous structure, a Brownfield can raise the property values of an area while introducing sustainable principles.

There are more than 400,000 Brownfields in the United States. You can find out more about how to redevelop one for your needs from the National Brownfield Association, at brownfieldassociation.org, or from their bimonthly publication *Brownfield News*.

# Energy Options

Along with finding a location, you will early on want to determine your energy needs and how you hope to fulfill them. If you are leasing, you may not have an option. I use the term "hope" because you may not have the initial funding to switch from an on-the-grid traditional means of power to a renewable means of power.

**Smart Tip** Tip...

Ever hear of fly ash? Fly ash is the fine residue powder byproduct from coal-fired electric generating plants. For building purposes, fly ash can be a great substitute for the less environmentally-friendly Portland Cement, most commonly found in concrete. Using 50 percent fly ash instead of Portland Cement will create a greener concrete that will be just as solid and dependable as traditional concrete.

It's important to keep in mind that options such as solar power will save a business money in the long term. And it's also worth keeping in mind that passive solar energy is an inexpensive means of lowering your energy expenditures. Therefore, let's start with the passive solar energy option, which you want to keep in mind when leasing, building, or renovating a location.

Passive heating and cooling is essentially a means of utilizing the heat from the sun, or blocking it, in an effort to control the temperature in your facility. Since sunlight does not require installation and is available in all parts of the world, it is the planet's leading source of energy. The concept of passive solar energy centers around having a strategy to maximize or minimize the amount of sunlight for heat, rather than depending on traditional fossil fuel-based energy sources. It can be a simple and very cost-effective manner of creating a green environment while also keeping your energy bills low in the process.

If you are building a new structure, or renovating your current one, you can position windows or add a sunroof to maximize the amount of heat you will let in. The concept is to let in heat during the warmest times of day and then "seal the envelope," as they say—shut all doors and windows—to keep the warm air in the space as it gets cooler. Conversely, in a warmer climate, you would open windows and a skylight during cooler hours and then seal in the cool air during warmer parts of the day. Shading can also be used effectively to minimize the heat while also being maneuvered to allow heat in when necessary. Operable skylights are particularly advantageous for passive cooling and heating. Opening a skylight allows the heat to rise out of the building; the escaped air then needs to be replaced, so it is pulled in from the outside creating natural convection and making the room cooler.

Another key to your heating will be both the colors used in the room, some of which draw heat more than others, and the flooring. If, for example, you have south facing windows that let the sun in, you can install the right type of flooring to help you heat the room. To do this, you will want to have a thermal mass, which is any material with the capacity to store heat, such as concrete or stone.

**Smart Tip**

In a sample survey taken by the National Small Business Association, which represents 150,000 small firms, they found that 73 percent would invest more in energy-saving products and services if energy prices continue to rise. Some 76 percent felt that cutting energy costs would boost profits.

You can also focus attention on cross-ventilation and the direction of prevailing winds, which can be used to bring in cooler air during the nighttime by opening specific windows.

For all buildings looking to utilize passive solar energy, it is important that you are able to maintain an air-tight building in order to capture, and then maintain, a temperature level inside the facility. High-efficiency windows, together with R-2000 levels of insulation and airtight construction allow passive solar heating to cover a large proportion of heating needs in many locations.

If, with the help of an environmentally proficient architect, designer, builder, or contractor, you can design a means by which the temperature is largely regulated by controlling the amount of hot and cold air in the facility, you will have achieved a means of passive solar heating/cooling. Another option you can consider, if you are getting too much heat, is to cool the roof of your building by using materials to make a more reflective surface, rather than one that absorbs heat. Plants can help keep a roof cool, while providing a natural green environment. Of course before planting, you'll need to make sure your roof is waterproofed and that you've done the necessary prep work prior to installing planters. Ford Motor Company's River Rouge Plant in Dearborn, Michigan, serves as a grand example of what plants can do—they feature 42,000 square meters of plants—while Silvercup Studios in New York City sports some 35,000 square feet of greenery above the television and film studio.

# Solar Panels and Wind Turbines

Two primary means of renewable energy are solar panels and wind turbines. The hope is that someday in the near future more businesses (and homes) will be utilizing these two means of generating power and less traditional power sources. One encouraging sign is that the government provides rebates and tax incentives for the use of renewable energy.

In order to utilize solar power, you will need to have an assessment, or audit, done to determine if such energy will be possible for your business. Some areas get more sunlight than others making it easier to utilize solar panels. Roger Strong, of Solar Wind Power introduced in Chapter 2, notes that readings known as "sun hours" can range from 3 to 7.5, the higher in areas such as the Mohave Desert. "We utilize solar maps of the United States which illustrate areas of lower and higher sun ratings," adds Strong, a renewable energy consultant.

Companies in the solar energy business will help you determine whether solar panels will be effective and a cost saver for your business. The panels themselves are rather inexpensive and have become more aesthetically pleasing in recent years. The type of structure will also factor into the equation. While most businesses do not go 100 percent solar, you can make a serious dent in your energy bills by going 25 to 50 percent solar. For example, if you run on solar power during just the higher rate hours as charged by your traditional energy server, you can save more money.

To measure the amount of electricity you are using, you will use what is called Net metering, which is now allowed in most states. This is a means of determining how much electricity you are using from the grid (or your electric company) and how much is being used from your solar panels. Power can come from the solar panels and be used first. Then the remaining needs are switched to the grid. If there's extra solar power, it goes back to the grid and turns the meter backwards.

So how much energy will you need? This will be determined by an assessment of your energy usage. If, as a small business, you use 1,300 kilowatt hours per month, then, at $9 per watt, your solar system, including installation and equipment, would run $11,700 before rebates and tax credits (9 x 1,300). This will vary depending on your needs.

Since all of the technical work is done by solar professionals, they can ultimately tell you how feasible solar power is for your place of business and then, in conjunction with the experts, you can determine how much cost savings you will see while benefiting the environment.

The other popular option is wind turbine power, which means windmills using the energy of the wind to power your business. You can either have wind turbines set up near your business or be part of a wind turbine farm.

Today, you'll find an increasing number of wind turbine-powered businesses in the United States, although far fewer than there should be considering the tremendous advantages of this low cost means of generating power.

Not unlike solar power, wind turbine power will be more effective in some areas than others. Coastal areas that get more wind will be more likely locations for wind turbines than most urban areas where large structures cut down on the wind.

Again, not unlike solar power, the conditions will need to be just right. "We look for at least five meters per second for average annual wind speed, which is about 11.2 miles per hour" says Roger Strong. He also points to the importance of wind speed. "If you compare 10 miles per hour to 12 miles per hour you can see a significant difference. The output from wind is measured by the cube of the wind speed, so 10 cubed versus 12 cubed is a 70 percent difference in power," explains Strong, adding that areas with above-average wind speed can make exponentially more power while areas below 5 mph generally cannot justify the cost.

While windmill height should generally be 30 feet higher than the surrounding buildings or trees within a 500-foot radius, there are also small boxes with small propellers that actually fit into the building, which can match the aesthetics of some businesses more easily. They are, however, less effective than the larger windmills, which are excellent, and often blend right into the landscape in rural locations.

Typically wind turbines for a business will cost anywhere from $6,000 to $20,000, so you will need to have enough startup money to get these environmentally friendly sources of power off the ground, so to speak. Once again, you will need to call in experts to determine whether or not wind power will work for your business.

Renewable energy sources are excellent ways to establish your commitment to the planet, while setting up long term means of saving money. The Solar America Initiative (SAI) is accelerating the development of photovoltaic (also known as PV or solar electricity) technologies with the goal of making solar electricity from PV cost competitive with conventional grid electricity by 2015.

# 5

# Business Equipment, Furniture, and Figuring Out Your Costs

Green businesses, like all businesses, need "green" to get started. Launching a business takes some capital, whether it's a few hundred dollars to start an organic business from home or a few hundred thousand dollars to purchase and renovate a Brownfield into an environmentally sound factory.

Most businesses will start out somewhere in between, and you will need to factor in startup costs along with the necessary operating costs of running your business on a monthly basis. Each business has specific requirements, along with some general business needs, which we will discuss here. You will need to do research to determine the costs of supplies, equipment, and inventory and then determine how much of each you will need to get started. In some areas going green will cost a little more up front but will pay off down the road. In other cases, you can save money, and the environment, right off the bat.

# Startup Costs

As the title implies, these are the costs that help you launch your business. Many will be one-time costs, while some will be the beginning of ongoing costs. For example, you will pay two months' rent up front, but then begin paying monthly. Startup costs will include all necessary licenses and permits to start your business, the cost of setting up a website; initial marketing and publicity expenses; office furnishings, business equipment, inventory (for retailers); a couple months of rent, or your down payment if you are buying a building or land on which to build.

For manufacturing you may need specialized equipment to create your products. For a retail business, you may need various types of display racks, possibly freezers or even mannequins. Regardless of what you need specifically for your business, you will need some standard goodies, such as computers, printers, and a reliable phone system.

# Computer Considerations

It's very rare to find a business today that does not utilize computers in some capacity. Whether it is for basic bookkeeping and e-mails or it's the backbone of your entire enterprise, you'll need computer equipment. In such a broad category, it's impossible to discuss the myriad of possibilities, ranging from one Blackberry to an elaborate network of twenty or more desktops. You can, however, think green in your computer shopping (and use).

First, keep in mind that laptops are better energy savers than desktops. Next, as is the case with nearly all equipment and appliances, you should look for Energy Star models. According to Energy Star's computer requirements (as of early 2008) the latest models are expected to save consumers and businesses more than $1.8 billion in energy costs over the next five years and prevent greenhouse gas emissions equal to the annual emissions of 2.7 million vehicles. These computers have lead-free circuitry and components, means of keeping the power supply cooler, and are designed to waste less power than their predecessors.

You can check out wattage used by looking at the specs for most computers and even do comparisons on various computer-oriented websites. Since most desktops use roughly 100 watts you want to look for the new breed of eco-friendly computers that use less than 75 watts while in use, less than 50 watts while idle, and 4 watts in sleep mode. When looking at laptops, you should look for models using less than 35 watts when in use, less than 15 watts in idle, and 2 watts when in sleep mode. Once upon a time your PC would run on full power at all times; that is no longer the case. Greener models switch to sleep mode when you are not using the computer, and even on older models, you can usually set the computer for sleep mode. This is far better than those fancy screen savers, which were major energy wasters.

In a highly competitive field you can be sure that along with the latest version of Apple's MacBook, you will find a wide range of emerging green models if you stay on top of the latest in computer technology from *PC Magazine*, *Computer World*, or other leading sources.

As of 2008, Zonbu Desktop Mini, the Zonbu notebook and Everex gPC VIA., Dell's Optiplex 755 and Latitude D630, Toshiba's Tecra A9-S9013, HP's Compaq dc7800 and the bare bones model dc5800 are among the latest in greener computers. Keep in mind that by the time you are done reading this page, newer models may have come out. Also keep in mind that newer models may cost more for features you don't really need, so pricing the recent previous model may be advantageous. Of course if you are one of those businesses that does not need the latest system, you can also purchase a previously owned model inexpensively, keeping one more computer from ending up in landfill.

The reuse of technology is becoming an important part of saving the vast amount of waste on the planet, and a green office can benefit if the computer needs are met by a computer from a recent year rather than a brand new model. Many small offices, and home offices, have done quite well with computers purchased from, or simply provided by, a friend, neighbor, relative, or business acquaintance who needed to purchase a more updated model for their line of work (or because they love the energy-wasting computer games).

While desktops are still very much in vogue for many businesses, laptops are adding a degree of mobility for millions of business owners and employees. Models range from under $1,000 to the higher end at $3,000+. When shopping for a laptop, look for something that is light but sturdy enough to withstand some bouncing around as you travel. Try out the trackball and look at the size of the screen—you need to feel comfortable. Popular laptops and notebooks can be found from Dell, Hewlett Packard, Compaq, Toshiba, IBM, Sony, Gateway, Fujitsu/Fuji, Acer, eMachines, and Apple.

Since laptops consume five times less energy than desktop PCs, they are becoming the choice of the new computer generation. As a business owner, laptops also allow you some flexibility in setting up your office, since people can move around, if necessary, or share work stations. Most laptops now include options for dual-core processors, and some even squeeze in two video cards in a Scalable Link Interface (SLI) configuration. If you are still dead set on buying a desktop, you can consider Small Form Factor Desktops, which are now an option from several leading computer makers. They are smaller, and require less energy than the traditional desktops. HP Pavilion Slimline S3330f and the HP Compaq DC7800 are among the latest in this PC series.

## Dollar Stretcher

It's always a good idea to get the extended warranty with a computer, especially a laptop because of the potential for more wear and tear. Consider the warranty costs when making your purchasing decision and go for two years beyond the warranty you get from the company. Most business do not need to upgrade computers more frequently than once every three years.

Also, when shopping for a desktop or laptop, keep an eye out for what are called "bundled extras," while browsing and comparing prices. Intrinsically necessary items like software, ink cartridges, and various peripherals can be part of a deal that might cost several hundred dollars if purchased separately. However, don't be sold on things you don't need, and ask for recycled possibilities since many companies are using recycled parts in their models.

The other means of making your computer use green from day one, is to start out by having computer policies in place, such as not leaving the machine on for hours while you are not using it. Also, opt for sleep mode when away from it.

For your sake, policies can include computer sharing. This means you will not need a computer for every single employee but can, instead, have two people alternate schedules and share one computer. Other policies might include looking for software or downloading programs that do not require high-end graphics. Also keep in mind that your monitor should be of the LCD variety, which is most likely what you will see advertised and on the sales floor (or manufacturer website) since CRT monitors are becoming a thing of the past. LCD monitors use less energy.

Of course software will also make a difference in energy use. Elaborate software with plenty of graphics can demand more energy expenditure than software with fewer bells and whistles. Today, the once "packaged" software products are offered directly over the web. Microsoft, for example, offers paperless options through sharing technology, which can be accessed online with passwords. Integrated with Microsoft Office 2008 are two systems, Groove and Office Live Workspace, both of which create a virtual sharing experience that creates a network environment for users who can see and make changes to each other's work. Another Microsoft software application, Live Meetings, allows numerous people to connect via virtual meeting technology, saving not only paper but, more significantly, travel. While face-to-face meetings cannot be eliminated, especially for the small business owner, it is not always easy or practical to meet with suppliers or even staff personnel who are at a different location. "One of the biggest concerns today of small-business owners is the price of gas," says Bill Rielly, Marketing Director for Microsoft Small and Midsize Businesses. "For pitching a new customer or talking to a contractor, it's a way to have a focused conversation without having to be face to face," adds Rielly of the electronically distributed software. It's also worth noting that the move by Microsoft and other companies to electronic software is a huge plus for the environment, saving on the packaging and shipping of software programs.

Even the much maligned Windows Vista has now come of age thanks to hours of retooling, and it, too, has gone green using sleep mode and hibernate to shut down power when not in use. "In a study, we found that for every ten computers that are upgraded to Vista, the environmental impact is the equivalent to taking one car off the road," adds Rielly.

# Printers and Eco-Friendly Ways of Using Them

There is a move toward eco-friendly printers, and companies like Hewlett Packard are taking the environmental concerns seriously by utilizing recycled parts in their latest models. Roughly 83 percent of the plastic in HP's D2545 printer is made from recycled plastics, while its packaging is 100 percent recyclable. In addition, the new printer uses the HP 60 black cartridges, which are made with 75 percent recycled plastic. Nokia, among other companies are introducing greener printers.

While energy-efficient models will cut down on energy expenditure, and recycled parts minimize that which is headed to landfill, the greenest printer may be the one that you use

## Smart Tip

*Tip...*

Want to draw more customers to your location? Find a cartridge recycling location in you area ... then put up a sign that customers can bring in cartridges to be recycled and you will give them the money for the recycled cartridges and take them in to the recycling location. If you position your mini-in-store recycling center near some impulse buys or in a place where they will pass some of your hottest selling items, who knows, drawing them in to the store might also prompt a sale. Other stores do this with batteries and other recyclable items. It's good for business and for the environment.

sparingly, so as not to waste paper. Printing on both sides will also cut paper use in half. Printers like the HP6122 Ink Jet can be had for under $200 and print quickly on both sides. Also, sending messages, memos, documents, and even manuscripts electronically, rather than printing hard copies, can be a major energy saver. While offices will need hard copies of invoices and contracts, you can minimize your need for hard copies by prioritizing what does and does not need to be printed. In addition, you can buy remanufactured laser toner, or ink, cartridges. And, when you are finished with your printer cartridges, you can recycle them for a longer life.

# Telephone Systems

The next "must have" on your list of startup costs is a telephone system that you can rely on. While phone systems today can be elaborate, you can save yourself expense and energy waste by simply going with the features you need. Too many business owners allow themselves to get suckered into buying a more elaborate, hence more complicated, telephone system, than they really need. Think "user friendly" when buying a phone system and remember the size of the business—sometimes small and simple is better. Also, utilize voice mail over answering machines. Voice mail is more professional for a business and saves energy as well. You will also typically have a cell phone or two for business use. Today, people are buying new cell phones at an alarming rate, fulfilling a need for the latest and greatest features. The problem is that cell phones are also discarded at an alarming rate: It is estimated that roughly 120 million cell phones are being retired each year in the United States. Since less than 3 percent are ever actually used by someone else, most end up in closets, drawers, or somewhere in the home, gathering dust. However, discarded cell phones are also ending up in landfill, and account for nearly 65,000 tons of toxic waste annually. It is important to get into the habit of recycling electronics, which includes cell phones, along with printer cartridges. There are a growing number of recycling centers springing up for cell phones. This is another area in which you can serve as a drop-off center and attract potential customers.

You can check out e-cycling cell phones at New Tech Recycling, newtechrecycling.com, Recellular at recellular.com/recycling, or find recycling locations at Eco-Cell at eco-cell.org/locate_recycler.asp.

# Other Equipment

There are plenty of other possible pieces of equipment, some of which can be greener through energy-efficient technology, which usually means not wasting electricity when not in actual use. You also want technology that does not emit toxins into the air. Of course, in many cases, the best way to utilize any equipment in an environmentally friendly manner is not to use it unless necessary. Here are a few of the many potential office items with some basic green thinking that can become your business policy.

- *Fax machines.* Unnecessary. If you use a fax software program, you can save on paper by having faxes go directly to your computer. You also eliminate "junk" faxes and another piece of equipment using energy and ending up as landfill. Many businesses are finding minimal need for fax machines.
- *Shredders.* If you must shred paper, then use it for your shipping needs.
- *Digital cameras.* Digital cameras are more environmentally friendly than their traditional counterparts because they do not involve photo processing chemicals that are discarded and are harmful to the environment. You can enhance their eco-attributes by using rechargeable batteries. Be careful, however, not to overload photos onto your computer or you will slow it down.
- *Calculators.* There are plenty of good solar models available.
- *Copiers.* Almost everyone leases their copiers today. Many are multi-purpose machines, with printing, scanning, and the ability to send materials directly to and from your PC network. Some models, such as Panasonic's C-3 series, warm up very quickly (in 15 seconds) and allow you to shut down the machine when not in use, thus saving energy. Before leasing a copier read the lease agreement carefully.

# Greener Office Supplies

Binders and paper products, including envelopes, can typically be found made from 30 to 75 percent recycled materials. Refillable pens, pencils from high-quality wood, markers from nontoxic materials, and other such supplies are all available today from various suppliers. Also remember not to over order and to keep track of what you have in house. Too much waste is the result of simply misusing and even losing supplies.

"We use 100 percent post-consumer recycled paper and have 95 percent recycled content in our furniture, some of which is made from wheat straw," says Chris Bartle, founder of the California based Evergreen Group LLC, a sustainable business brokerage dedicated to helping business owners buy and sell green businesses.

As you get into the habit of buying and using recycled products, it's a good idea to spread the word by letting vendors and customers know that you are dong so in hopes that you set an example for other businesses and individuals.

## Read the Fine Print

**W**hile minimizing the use of paper is a goal of most eco-efficient businesses, there will be a need for some paper in any business situation. Again, you need to have the green mindset. Look for paper with a high percentage of postconsumer recycled content rather than paper from 100 percent virgin pulp. While you may not always have the choice (depending on where you shop) you can ask if "recycled" means from post-consumer recycled content or not. If not, and you have no other choice, buy the paper recycled from 100 percent virgin pulp. The difference is that you are buying paper that was discarded in the production process, which is better than having it go to waste. However, paper that has been used by consumers and recycled keeps the product in the lifecycle. You also want to buy processed chlorine-free paper.

# Green Office Furniture

Your basic office needs will typically include a desk and/or workstation as well as an ergonomically designed chair, plus storage and filing space. The more customers and clients you anticipate visiting your office, the more you will need to design to impress, as well as for practical purposes. Conversely, an office in the back of a retail store or a manufacturing facility or a home office from which you will rarely entertain visitors needs to focus primarily on function rather than form.

There are two approaches you'll want to take when shopping for office furniture in general. First you want to be cost effective and second, you want to focus on sustainability in the products you choose. There are plenty of environmentally friendly furniture options. Of course you may be wondering how your office furniture affects the environment while it sits quietly in its designated location. First, the production of office furniture depletes the forests and mineral reserves. Second, the making of such furniture releases emissions from chemicals into the air. Finally, some furniture continues to emit volatile organic compounds into the air in your office, causing indoor air pollution.

To be cost effective, you will need to consider what you need in order to present a "look" and what you need simply for functionality. For the latter, you can explore previously owned items and even scout around to see if you have something at home that, with a little work, might fit the bill. Recycling furniture is a marvelous means of helping the environment while keeping your costs down. Considering that U.S. companies buy about 3 million desks, 16.5 million chairs, 4.5 million tables, and 11 million file cabinets each year, it is very likely that you will be able to cash in on someone's former furnishings and, with a little refurbishing, make them look brand new.

Here are some eco-friendly tips for buying office furniture:

1. Look for office furniture made from recycled plastics, paper, wood, and/or steel. Seek out post-consumer recycled content.
2. Look for products that are free of volatile organic compounds (VOC).
3. Consider products made from bamboo, such as a Kyoto Bamboo Desk or bamboo flooring, which is becoming more popular.
4. Look for companies making furniture from sustainably harvested woods, and look for Forest Stewardship Counsel (FSC) certified woods.
5. Seek out products made with bio-based, or nontoxic materials, and with glues, paints, foams, and other ingredients that don't give off noxious odors.
6. Look for environmental certifications such as LEED certified or certification from Greenguard.

In an effort to appeal to the eco-culture of the modern business office, it is becoming much easier to find greener office furniture. Leading companies, including Herman Miller and the Knoll Group, are designing furniture that meets high standards in health, safety, and sustainability. Both companies deal largely in wood products and have made strong efforts to work with producers with best overall forestry practices.

Other companies, such as Guilford of Maine and Steelcase are utilizing a wide range of recycled products, including recycled soda bottles, in creating their new lines of office furniture.

From a buyer's perspective, it is easier than ever to visit websites and get the lowdown on what types of materials are included and the chemical makeup of the end products. You can also see if the products contain recycled materials and can be recycled after their usefulness to you.

Some of the many green office shopping sites include the Green Office at greenoffice.com, which will tell you what level of green you'll get with each product, Green Office Projects at greenofficeprojects.com, and Ergonomic Home at ergonomichome.com, which has a green office section. You might also get some ideas from visiting Open Plan Systems at openplan.com, a company that re-manufactures furniture, especially Herman Miller workstations and basically turns old into new. By cleaning and repainting, using low VOC coatings and finishes, and adding new environmental fabrics, this Richmond, Virginia, company can provide low-cost office options that look great.

# Chairs and Lighting

Two areas of significance, when furnishing your office, which are often overlooked are chairs and lighting. Both are a key factor in the health and well-being of your employees, and both can also be green. Ergonomically designed chairs are a must for long hours on the computer. Back and neck pain, carpal tunnel syndrome, and other ailments are very often the result of bending, straining, or reaching from chairs that are not designed for your work needs. And, many such chairs are made from recycled materials. While you can skimp on filing cabinets by repainting some older ones, don't skimp on quality office chairs or you may find yourself paying for it down the road at your chiropractor's office.

There are three ways to light your space. First, you need some general lighting for your facility, illuminating the overall space. Next you need workspace-specific lighting, also known as task-specific lighting, which is very important for working closely on projects. Finally, you should include some natural lighting from our old friend, the sun. In fact, large windows with unencumbered views can allow you to use your general overhead lighting less and save money. And you can still maintain a cool environment if you recall what we discussed earlier about passive cooling, or letting cool air in at night, sealing the envelope, or locking it in for the daytime.

The type of lighting used is also a key to being more energy efficient. In fact, the International Energy Agency published in a report that a global switch to efficient lighting systems would cut the world's energy cost by 10 percent. Traditional incandescent bulbs emit more carbon emissions and use more energy. With that in mind, LED (light-emitting diode) and CFL (compact fluorescent lamp) bulbs have become the bulbs of choice for the new eco-friendly culture.

One significant difference offered by these newer bulbs is the amount of hours of light. For example, an LED bulb has a lifespan of roughly 60,000 hours, while a CFL bulb provides 10,000 hours. Incandescent bulbs last only about 1,500 hours. LED lights save energy because they do not have a filament that needs to be heated up (as in incandescent bulbs). In other words, the electrical energy used is going directly to generating light, rather than heat and then, subsequently, light. CFL bulbs radiate a different light spectrum from that of incandescent lamps but can usually be used in the same light sockets. You'll also find compact fluorescent tubes (CFTs) which are the fluorescent

## Smart Tip

Did you know that if you have 20 to 30 incandescent lightbulbs in your house, averaging 6-hours a day of use, you cuold replace them all with CFL bulbs and reduce your annual $CO_2$ output by upward of 2.3 metric tons in a year, which is roughly 10 percent of the average American household's annual carbon footprint.

versions. A CFL or CFT contains a gas-filled tube and, typically, an electronic ballast. Electric current flowing through this ballast, with the gas inside, creates ultraviolet light. This powers the phosphor coating in the tube creating the light that you see. This process also requires less energy than the incandescent light bulb, saving you on your energy costs by as much as 66 to 75 percent if you were to replace all of your lighting with CFLs. It should also be noted the CFLs, as well as LEDs, do not emit as much heat as incandescent bulbs, lowering your need for cooling your office, retail, or factory space.

Of course basic lighting policies such as not leaving lights on when nobody is in the office and even having light sensors to shut off lights in copy rooms or other areas when they are not being used also helps keep lighting bills lower.

# Green Printing

Brochures, special mailing, promotional materials, receipts, invoices, and other printed matter will likely be a part of your business. While the paperless office is a nice idea, it remains impractical in the real world.

You can, however, make a difference with the right ink on your printed materials. While often overlooked, the use of ink and printed matter is among the most significant contributors to global warming and the environmental damage to our planet.

In fact, the third largest contributor to pollution in the industrialized world is the paper/pulp industry. This does not even take into account the many trees that are destroyed in the papermaking process.

Along with the use of recycled paper, as mentioned earlier, and Processed Chlorine Free (PCF) paper, which is made without the use of chlorine or chlorine derivatives, you can look for ink that is not petroleum based. Today it is easy to find ink made from a soy, vinegar, or vegetable oil base, all of which have fewer volatile organic compounds (VOC) than their traditional petrolium-based ink counterparts.

The other, and simplest, way to be eco-friendly when it comes to printed materials is to order what you need. It is very common for businesses that have 200 attendees at a seminar to run 300 copies of the program, or for 2,000 employees, to run 3,000 copies of the corporate handbook. Overruns are a tremendous waste of paper and printing materials. Consider electronic means of disseminating information whenever possible, printing on both sides, and looking for other ways to minimize your printing needs.

For more on green printing, you can check out Green Printer at greenprinter.com or Quad Graphics at qg.com.

# Website Designers

One area you will need to consider carefully is your website. In today's world, a small business can have a major presence and compete with much larger businesses by having a first–rate website. Only if you are very well versed in website building should you create it yourself.

From $1,000 to $100,000, you can have a website designed to your liking. Typically, such a job should be in the $2,000 to $10,000 range depending on how elaborate your site needs to be and what you are using it for. The three main purposes of a business website are to:

1. Advertise and promote your business
2. Provide information and knowledge about your products and services
3. Sell goods and/or services.

Therefore, you need to determine what it is that your site will feature. Obviously, if your business is strictly web based, you will need to focus heavily on all three. However, if you are opening an organic restaurant, you will primarily need to advertise and promote on one page and provide some information, such as a menu and directions on another. A simple two- or three-page site should be easy and inexpensive to set up.

While you cannot steal someone else's site, you can get ideas from tons of other sites, which is exactly what you should do before looking for a web designer. This will allow you to see what type of sites you like best and show them to a designer. It will also help you find a designer whose work meets your needs.

Since every business needs a website today, here are 15 tips to getting yours started:

1. *Think reader friendly, as in easy on the eyes.* Weird color combinations and crowded pages are very hard for viewers, especially when you consider how many people are now looking at the internet on small screens on their hand-held devices.
2. *Remember that less can be more.* White space is not your enemy.
3. *Set the tone of the business.* A business selling toys or services for kids, such as party planning, should have a cheery, upbeat, even somewhat colorful style, while a consulting service will have a more sedate image. Match the image to the business.
4. *Make it clear what your business does (or sells).* Too many business websites provide "solutions" and are, therefore, very ambiguous. Other companies try to sell or promote everything under the sun, which gets extremely confusing for

buyers. Go with your strengths upfront. Customers can always look further for more information.

5. *Make sure the site is designed for easy navigation.* Nobody likes to click again and again and again and again to get to what they are looking for. If a customer doesn't see what he or she is looking for in one or two (maybe three) clicks, he or she is gone.

6. *Have an "About Us" page and be transparent.* Nameless, faceless websites in an age of security concerns, do not win people over.

7. *Make sure you have a clearly written privacy policy.* Read those on other sites and have an attorney help you draft one using similar language. Make sure you adhere to the policy.

8. *Use fewer bells and whistles and more content.* Gimmicks, gadgets, slow-loading graphics, etc., all use more energy and waste people's time. They were once new and exciting but have become a negative, especially when trying to be "greener"

9. *Promote your greenness.*

10. *Update your website often.* Stale sites do not entice return visitors.

11. *Make your site interactive if possible, through reader polls, contests, and other means.*

12. *Use "Forward to a friend" links so that your readers can help you advertise your site by doing it for you.*

13. *Provide some crisp, clear, fresh content so people have a reason to come back.*

14. *Make sure the site works by doing periodic checkups on all links.*

15. *Ask for feedback and suggestions and actually read and respond to them.*

To get your site up and running, you will need a hosting company, one that specializes in business, and work with a designer who has other sites that he or she can show you. Make sure your designer has the same vision as you have before he or she starts designing. Finally, look at the site in various stages before you see the finished product.

# Startup Costs Revisited

There's no set formula for determining how much it will cost to start a business. The field is too broad, there are too many possibilities and types of possible businesses. For your purposes, you will want to make a list of each of the office equipment, furniture, and office supplies (including pens and paper, which have many recyclable options) you will need, as well as having your website designed and built. Also look at your initial advertising and marketing needs and so on.

Use the Startup Expenses Worksheet for a breakdown. You can fill in costs as they pertain to your business needs. Remember, the more creative you are at recycling older items, such as furniture, and the better you are at gauging what you actually will need and use, rather than overbuying (another problem that leads to waste and ultimately landfill), the better off you will be from an expense standpoint.

## Startup Costs Worksheet

| Item | Startup Cost |
| --- | --- |
| Computer system(s) with printer(s) | $ |
| Business equipment, both general, such as a copier, and industry specific, such as your dental chair | $ |
| Office furniture for one or many offices (cubicles can work too, especially with eco-friendly cubicle designs made from recycled materials) | $ |
| Website design and promotion | $ |
| Internet access | $ |
| Software (general and business specific) | $ |
| Electronic credit card processing if you are selling items or services | $ |
| Market research costs | $ |
| Telephone system, including cell phones and voice mail (also a call center if necessary to fulfill orders) | $ |
| Stationery and office supplies | $ |
| Shipping and packaging materials | $ |
| Postage | $ |
| Initial inventory for retailers | $ |

# Startup Costs Worksheet

| Item | Startup Cost |
|---|---|
| Business licenses and any other necessary requirements for doing business, such as a zoning variance if necessary | $ |
| First two months' rent or down payment for purchase | $ |
| Business and property inspections | $ |
| Initial utilities installation costs (which can be renewable energy as discussed earlier) | $ |
| Remodeling or any contracting necessary | $ |
| Vehicles for transporting goods or mobile services (look for hybrids or trucks running on biodiesel) | $ |
| Landscaping and/or architectural needs | $ |
| HVAC System (this, too, can be energy efficient) | $ |
| Initial advertising and marketing budget (don't skimp here) | $ |
| Lawyer and accounting fees to help you get started | $ |
| **Total Startup Expenses** | $ |

These are some of the most common and significant business startup costs. Clearly, such costs can run the gamut depending on the size and complexity of the business you are starting. Your goal is to determine your business size and scope and then research a reasonable startup cost to launch such a business. A small homebased crafts business might cost $2,000 to launch needing only craft supplies and a means of marketing your products. A home-cleaning business might cost $10,000 to get off the ground, while a retail store might be in the $50,000 to $100,000 range. A larger manufacturing business, with specialized equipment could run you several hundred thousand dollars. The point is, you will look at the possibilities and determine what size business you can feasibly open, manage, and run.

# Operating Costs

Remember, along with startup costs, you will have monthly operating costs, which may include:

- Rent or mortgage payments
- Utilities
- Phone bills
- Heat and water bills
- Buying/restocking inventory
- Supplies
- Employee salaries and wages
- Employee benefits
- Website payments
- Advertising, promotion, and marketing costs
- Bookkeeping
- Legal and accounting fees
- Dues and subscriptions
- Security
- Maintenance (cleaning service)
- Postage and shipping
- Business travel and entertainment
- Repairs
- Commissions
- Insurance
- Taxes
- Miscellaneous

You will need to determine how much falls into each or all of these categories on a monthly basis. For areas such as repairs, which you may need only twice a year at $600 a pop, you would simply take the total, $1,200, and spread it out monthly at $100 per month. This way you can determine how much you will need on a monthly basis to launch and maintain your operation. Since most businesses take at least one year, and often as many as three years, to see a profit, you'll want to look for a point in time in which you foresee at least enough money to cover your expenses.

If, for example, your startup costs for a small business come to $50,000 and you see that it will cost you $8,000 per month to run the business, then you are looking at $146,000 to make it through the first year, or $242,000 to get through two years, some of which will hopefully come from running the business with some income coming in.

In the next chapter we will look at some means of gathering the necessary money to launch your green business. Getting the "green" for going green—a nice concept.

# Getting the Green to
## Go Green

Starting a business means having capital available. Whether it's $5,000 from your last bonus check that will start your part-time business, or $100,000 saved up for years for the express purpose of opening your own company, you will need to know that you are funded above and beyond the money you need to cover your living expenses. Going into great debt or sacrificing your home or the needs of your family is no way to start a business. Nor can you depend on the kindness of others to help you start. Sure, friends and family may help you out with chores, tasks, and even secondhand goods, especially in an effort to support the environment. But, there is no escaping the fact that it costs money (even a little bit) to make money.

Look at your numbers from the previous chapter. How much will you need in startup costs? How much to get through at least one year? Remember, you need to have cash available, not just for operating expenses but also for the many unexpected costs that will arise. Financing a business is not an easy proposition and separates the serious entrepreneurs from those with a dream but not the willingness to make it happen. If you are dreaming about a business that is potentially profitable while also benefiting the environment, you have two goals in mind and should have twice the incentive to go for the green, in both contexts.

# Green Financing

There are several means of generating money for a business. Utilizing your "green" angle may make it a little bit easier as you go, since more and more government and environmental agencies are eager to support green initiatives. Even lenders are becoming more receptive to business plans that include sustainability and waste management.

In fact, the Environmental Bankers Association (EBA), a nonprofit trade association founded in 1994 in an effort to bring greater awareness to environmental risk issues and the need for environmental risk management, reported that Citibank and CitiFinancial (both EBA members) are not only designing bank branches with sustainable features, but also are committed to addressing global change. CitiBank has pledged to reduce greenhouse gas emissions by 10 percent by 2011. What does this mean for you? Greener banks mean environmentally friendlier lending possibilities. For example, Wells Fargo & Company, as of mid 2008, have provided more than $1.5 billion in financing for LEED-certified green buildings with loans ranging from $10 million to $225 million for properties such as offices, apartments, and schools.

A recent program launched by Bank of America (BOA) put $20 billion dollars aside to finance companies creating low-emission technology over the next decade. Bank of America will change its underwriting criteria for commercial loans to include environmental factors, such as whether a business creates "sustainable products, services and technologies." Essentially, businesses creating less carbon output while making eco-friendly products will score higher on loan applications than those using an abundance of fossil fuels.

PNC Financial Services Group Inc., based in Pittsburgh, Pennsylvania, is another major supporter of green building and boasts 42 LEED-certified buildings, including its operational facilities in Pittsburgh and Wilmington, Delaware. They are also promoting sustainable building practices among loan officers and throughout the lending industry so that sustainability can be included in the underwriting of loans.

A smaller example of green lending comes from New Resource Bank in San Francisco, a niche lender since 2006 that focuses on a variety of green initiatives ranging from providing mortgages on green homes and commercial buildings to offering loans for green-oriented businesses.

> ## Green News
>
> Lenders are currently defining what environmental responsibility actually means. Nonetheless, they are looking more closely at businesses that are focused on sustainability, green business practices, clean technology, and cleaner energy.

While this does not mean that business loans are easy to get, it does mean that there is a much greater emphasis from banks and other lenders to include environmental criteria in the application process. Of course there are still no efficiency values or benchmarks that have been clearly established. However, greener buildings and companies are becoming more clearly visible and recognized by the U.S. Green Building Council, which has certified 1,129 commercial properties under their LEED rating system.

What all of this means is that if you shop around, you are more likely to find a lender who takes your green business ideas more seriously and gives you more points for your environmental plans than in the past. Corporate governance practices, including social responsibility and sustainable product finance, are rapidly becoming a growing concern for financial institutions, and environmental lending practices are incorporating many of these principles into their lending policies.

# Finding Funding

Obviously banks, credit unions, and lending institutions are the primary means of finding the funding you need to launch a business. Other means include private or angel investors and venture capitalists.

The key to any borrowing situation is to demonstrate that you are not a bad risk, especially when dealing with commercial lenders. Your credit rating needs to be high and you need to demonstrate that you will be able to pay back the loan promptly. Before you start on your quest for money, it's always a good idea to check on your credit score from the three major credit bureaus. This way you will know where you stand should you be seeking a loan.

▲

## Taking Credit

**C**ontact at least one of the big three credit bureaus for your credit scores.

- ❍ Equifax: (800) 685-1111, PO Box 740241, Atlanta, GA 30374; equifax.com
- ❍ Experian: (888) 397-3742, PO Box 2002, Allen, TX 75013, experian.com
- ❍ TransUnion: (800) 888-4213, PO Box 2000, Chester, PA 19022; transunion.com

Do this once, since the loan officers will also inquire and the more your credit ratings are checked, the more suspicious it can appear to lenders. Read over your ratings *very carefully*, since credit bureaus make more mistakes than you would ever imagine.

If your credit scores are not where you'd like them to be, start working on paying off any and all outstanding debts and get to a point where you can open a new credit card or take out a small loan and pay it back promptly, thus showing you are on solid financial ground. Do not seek out places that can magically repair bad credit. Remember, anything that seems too good to be true usually is a major risk and you are very likely to find yourself in a worse situation, since it's very unlikely that someone can turn around your bad credit unless they are handing you a check to pay it off. Even then, you still need to build up a track record of timely payments.

# The All-Important Business Plan

Your next step in starting a business is to draw up a business plan. This is valuable whether you are seeking capital or not, but a must if you are looking for a loan from a lending institution.

The prospect of writing a business plan can be intimidating. However, with all of the templates and samples available in books, articles, and on websites, you do not have to re-invent the wheel. Depending on your business needs, you can make your business plan as formal or informal as you want. Certainly, if you are approaching a major lending institution for a $100,000 loan, you will want to have a more elaborate and detailed plan than if you are going to a local bank, or a private lender for $5,000. Either way, however, your business plan needs to be a well-thought-out document detailing what you plan to do with your business idea and how it will be profitable. In essence, your business plan is a blueprint for your company's future.

There are actually two primary reasons for writing up such a plan. First, it will allow you to show lending institutions, or private lenders, that you have thought out this plan from every angle, that you have a complete picture of the business you are planning to start, including the finances that will be needed and how the money will be spent in each area, and what the projected return on the investment will be in one, three, five, and possibly even ten years down the road. It will also give you an opportunity to explain how your passion and concern for the environment will be represented in your business endeavor and how such environmental standards, policies, and practices will benefit the planet.

Your other primary reason for writing a business plan is that it serves as a guide for yourself, and for those involved in building and running the business. A good business plan is an ever-evolving document that can keep you on track, allowing you to see your progress, and can often help you determine whether there is or is not growth potential over time. You may look at your business plan and decide that everything is going better than schedule, thus allowing you to expand, perhaps by adding a new profit center. Conversely, your numbers may be lagging behind your projections. This might lead you to determine ways to improve upon the bottom line by making changes. In addition, you may see ways in which you can become more sustainable, save energy, and even utilize profits to explore eco-friendly initiatives.

To begin, you should look at the Center for Business Planning website on business plans at businessplans.org. You could also go to Palo Alto's bplans.com or the Small Business Administration's site, sba.org, and look up business plans. You can also ask other business owners that you know if you can peruse their business plans. Books available on the subject, such as David H. Bangs, Jr.'s *Business Plans Made Easy*, Tim Berry's *Plan-As-You-Go Business Plan*, Mike P. McKeever's *How to Write a Business Plan*, or Nik Kerner's *Creating a Business Plan: Your Dream Concept Made Real* can also be helpful.

Of course many older and more traditional plans won't include green elements, or perhaps very minimally. You, however, can work both a sustainability and waste management plan into your business plan as you proceed and include green marketing in your marketing section.

## Components of a Business Plan

Below are the areas included in most business plans. Some sections will incorporate more detail and in some cases your business plan will include additional sections. However, this is a basic overview of what you want to include. Most significantly, you want to think through each section very carefully and visualize how each aspect of your business will work.

## Table of Contents

This simply makes it easy for your readers to follow the subsequent plan.

## The Executive Summary

Although this comes first, it is often written last, after you have had the opportunity to think through the various areas of your business. It is here that you provide a one- or two-page summary of your business including the reasons why you are starting it—your goals, plans, and objectives for the business, the industry, and the environment. Here you will present your target audience, marketing plans and future expectations. This is, in fact, a summary that should entice potential investors to read further—it is the single most important aspect of a business plan and one that should provide a solid, factual basis for your business to succeed. It should NOT include a lot of hype, but instead feature a realistic view of what your business will be all about. Wow the reader with your business ideas rather than a lot of superlatives or vague promises.

## Industry Analysis

Researching this section of the business plan is a marvelous way for you to bone up on the industry, whatever it may be. Here, you describe the state of the industry at present and how your business will fit in. Also, describe how your green ideas can make an impact. By showing your knowledge of the industry, you will demonstrate that you have done your research and know what you are getting into. In addition, you'll want to show how the future looks in the industry. A bleak picture for upcoming years may start you questioning whether this is the right business to go into at the present time.

## Business or Operational Overview

Here, you will provide a comprehensive overview of your plans for the business. How will the business operate? What kind of business structure you will have? What resources will you need? Where will you be based? For example, you will operate the business from a home office in Traverse, Michigan, or a 3,200-square-foot warehouse just outside of Detroit? Explain the way your products will be made and distributed, how you will provide your services, and/or how you will interact with customers. Will they drive through and order from a clown's mouth or sit with your highly trained sales staff and select high-end items by appointment only? You can also include in this section how your business operations will be eco-friendly and sustainable. If you have a waste management plan, this is one place where you can work it into your plan of action. Demonstrating how your business will be ecologically viable is a big plus. Today, finding greener ways to implement business practices will be applauded by potential supporters.

## Marketing Plan

The marketing plan is an important aspect of your overall business and one that requires you to pay strict attention. How will customers, clients, and other businesses know about you, your products, and your services? What type of research and consumer marketing will you be doing to determine your best areas for sales? All types of marketing efforts should be included here. Gather as much background information as possible to support your demographic research. Finally, explain your plan for reaching the audience. Will you advertise? Use direct mail? The internet? Special promotions and coupons? If you have media contacts or know of publicists that will help you spread the word, also include that information in this section. The mere process of writing the marketing section will get you motivated to work on this important area. You can promote green marketing possibilities here as well, focusing on word of mouth and means of spreading the word that require little to no use of fossil fuels and energy expenditure.

## Competitive Analysis

This is obviously a very important part of the business plan. As much as you'd like to "trash" your competitors, you need to take the high road—or have a professional approach. Discuss all of your direct and indirect competition (meaning other similar businesses that could draw customers away from your company). Provide information on their businesses, including their prices along with areas in which they do well and areas in which they are lacking. Finally, use the information you have gathered on your competitors to show what you can improve upon and what will bring customers to you. This is your competitive edge and what separates the successful entrepreneurs from the wannabes. You can also include green ideas here that will make you more sustainable than your competitors. Again, your goal is not to go green simply to create a competitive edge, BUT it doesn't hurt to show that you are thinking in a direction that, perhaps, some of your competition is not.

## Management Team

If you are all alone, then this is a brief overview of why you are the man or woman for the job. A few paragraphs should do it, recounting your applicable business experiences. No, lenders and investors do not really care about the bake sale you ran in middle school or your Boy/Girl Scout awards—they want to see that you have some business background, particularly in dealing with clients and customers, since most businesses are centered around interpersonal relationships. Finance is another area that will spark their attention, along with bringing good ideas to fruition. Here you can include your environmental endeavors to date, as well as your applicable business skills and background. If you have other people going into business with you, this is where you list them; include a short bio and show exactly what they will bring to the business.

# Financial Software

To make your life much easier, there are a host of financial and accounting software packages available that can help you when working on your business plan and from that point forward. Most of these include customizable templates for financial forecasting such as break-even analysis, profit and loss statements, and cash-flow projections (which should all be part of your business plan).

- ○ Fundable Plans, fundableplans.com
- ○ Plan Magic, planmagic.com
- ○ Palo Alto, paloalto.com
- ○ QuickBooks, quickbooks.com
- ○ Peach Tree, peachtree.com

### *Financial Plan*

Another biggie, this is where you "show them the money," so to speak—or more specifically, how you plan to manage and utilize the funding that you get to launch, run, and show a profit from your business. Here, you will include all the financial information from starting up your green business to the projected profits. Use any charts and graphs necessary to illustrate how money will come in, how expenses will be handled, and what profits will ensue. Let your accountant help you with this part and try not to exaggerate or get carried away. Inaccurate financial projections are among the primary reasons why many businesses fail. Be cautious, conservative if necessary, and show estimates of how you will build your business.

It is also very important to make it clear how much funding you are seeking from any given lender, what the money will be used for and who else is backing your endeavor. While you may not have anyone else lined up, it is always a very good sign if you are putting up some of your own money. Lenders like to see that you are at least taking some of the risk.

You may also include supporting material at the end of the business plan along with your resume and any additional financial documents that support the business plan.

## Reviewing Your Business Plan

Before showing anyone your business plan, review it very carefully and do some rewriting. You want the plan to answer all of the possible questions that anyone could pose about the future of your business. If you cannot answer all questions posed, it means you have areas that you have not thought through. Reading your business plan a couple of times should afford you the opportunity to tie up all loose ends and make sure everything is included for a reason and all potential stumbling blocks to a smoothly operating business have been addressed.

This is where some business owners call in a consultant, or at least look for some guidance if they intend to use the business plan to accrue financing. While you can, and probably should, write your own business plan, you may want someone to review it and perhaps tweak it a bit to make it as eye-opening to potential investors as possible. Before hiring anyone, make sure they have some expertise in business plans, particularly in your genre, whether that is in retail, service or a manufacturing business. You also want someone who has good listening skills and hears what you are trying to say in your plan and not someone who is going to change everything to their way of thinking. Remember, this is your business so don't let someone steer you away from your goals. Another option is to have business owners whom you know personally give you some feedback. This should come from people you know well and trust.

In addition to the business side of your plan, you can work your way through all of the realistic environmental possibilities that you foresee in the short and long term. What goals can you aim for, not just for your business, but for the planet? How will being green affect your accounting, profit margin, and marketing? These are areas

## SCORE!!

While starting up a business and writing a business plan, you might want to look for a mentor to advise you. SCORE "Counselors to America's Small Business" is a nonprofit association that helps entrepreneurs such as yourself get started and grow a small business. The nationwide company provides free mentoring with SCORE (which stands for Service Corp of Retired Executives) volunteers, who are working and retired executives with experience and background in numerous types of businesses. Founded in 1964, SCORE volunteers, who now number over 10,500, have helped business owners all over the country and continue to do so on an ongoing basis. Based in Washington, DC, and a part of the Small Business Administration, SCORE can be reached at score.org, where you will find a wealth of information, or by calling (800) 634-0245 or (703) 487-3612. They've helped eight million small businesses get off the ground, so it's very likely that SCORE can be helpful to you.

you'll want to consider as you design a green business plan. Remember, the key is to carefully manage the "traditional" moneymaking aspects of your endeavor with the ways and means of doing things in an environmentally efficient and beneficial manner. In short, many companies design, make, and sell clothing successfully for a profit. Your business can do the same thing, using sustainable, organic materials, plus eco-friendly packaging and methods of marketing.

# Your Sustainability Plan

One of the best definitions of "sustainability" is "meeting the needs of the present without compromising the ability of future generations to meet their needs." With this in mind, you can consider drawing up a sustainability plan for your business so that you can demonstrate how you can operate without impinging upon the future of the planet . . . . or by having a very minimal negative impact, such as that caused by carbon emissions.

Among the components of a sustainability plan, can be your plan for power and utilities, which might include renewable energy. Alternative fuel options, energy conservation efforts, and working with local energy providers who have incentive plans or even rebates for saving energy may all be part of your overall energy use strategies.

Another area you might include is your means of production. How can you make products in a manner that minimizes waste and utilizes recycled or organic goods? Are you using eco-friendly materials in what you build? If so, include this in your sustainability plan.

Transportation and commuting is another area that you will likely want to touch upon. This includes ways in which you and your employees commute to and from work, as well as how you ship products. Ride-share programs, biking, and public transportation can all be encouraged to transport your staffers to and from the office while bio-fuels and hybrid vehicles can move your products from place to place in a greener manner.

Your sustainability plan should touch upon all areas of your business and demonstrate your plan for doing things in a greener way.

# Your Waste Management Plan

Included within your sustainability plan, or written separately, should be a discussion on how you plan to dispose of waste. The idea is to avoid landfill by:

- Recycling

## Consider Composting!

Composting is a process in which biodegradable material (which includes garden and kitchen waste) is converted, through the presence of oxygen from the air, into a stable material that can be applied to land and soil to improve and enrich the nutrient content. Another way of looking at it would be turning garbage into fertilizer for gardens, rather then sending it off to landfill.

Most compost is made up of food scraps, although some types of food and garbage will fit the needs of composting better than others. It is an excellent way of recycling natural ingredients. To learn about composting, check out The U.S. Composting Council at compostingcouncil.org.

- Reusing
- Redistributing waste

The term "waste" can be rather broad; one company's waste is another company's gold. For example, some of the waste products found on the grounds of New Belgium Brewery's facility are reused by other companies to make fish food. Another company utilizes algae found on New Belgium's 25 acres to help make bio-fuel. Likewise, discarded metals and woods have been reused, reshaped, and remodeled to become avante-garde furniture. Your waste plan can also include how you will save resources, which includes water conservation, landscape, and use of agriculture.

In the end, your plan should cover all aspects of your business and explain how debris and other types of "waste" will be collected, recycled, salvaged, and disposed of in your company.

# Personal Loans

If you are not looking at commercial lenders, or do not feel that you have either sufficient collateral or a credit rating that will impress such lenders, you can always look for a personal loan.

Some advisors will tell you that the ideal place to look for a personal loan is from the people you know best, such as family or friends. Others will recount horror stories of relationships gone very wrong. The key to borrowing from friends or family members is to make sure that they honestly respect your plans and ideas and are not doing it out of guilt, pity, or for any ulterior motive. You do not want to be beholden to anyone. You want this to be treated as a business deal and any lender should know that you fully intend to pay them back. You also want to borrow from people looking to help with financing without strings attached. If your great uncle decides that he has a great way for you to run the business, his loan may not be worth his conditions. Only you can discern whether or not the relationships in your life can withstand financial implications.

If you are looking for outside investors, you will want to polish that business plan and practice answering all possible questions regarding the plan. You also want to do your research and get to know something about the lender. You might find an angel investor to back your business venture. "Angels" are wealthy individuals who invest in projects to become wealthier and to be involved in a business. In many cases, they are retired or semi-retired and are investing, in part, because of their interest in the subject matter. For example, those who sink money into a new theater production aren't always expecting to see a bundle of money in return. They do, however, enjoy the theater. Therefore, if you can find someone who is a wealthy car enthusiast, you might be able to get some backing from then for your auto-detailing business. Perhaps you'll find someone who shares your concern for the environment and wants to support your development of an eco-friendly line of goods. Typically, finding such investors comes from looking around, networking, and seeking out a person, or a few people, who want to get in on the ground floor of a business that touches them in some manner. The only real concern on your part (besides having your attorney draw up the proper paperwork) is how much involvement the person wants to have in operating the business. While someone in this capacity may be a source of wisdom, you do not want them taking over your goals and dreams.

It is important when dealing with anyone lending you money that you have a clear understanding of the involvement of that backer in your business. You could have several backers, all of whom meet with you periodically to brainstorm. Conversely, you could have only a silent partner—or several—who lends money but is not at all involved in the business.

Determine which is best for you.

# Government Financing

The Small Business Administration (SBA) at sba.gov should be your first stop when looking for assistance from the government. They specialize in helping small-business owners who are getting started, offering many loan programs. Of course you can also look into government programs designed to support the type of business you are starting. For example, if your business is transportation, the United States

Department of Transportation offers short-term lending programs. Should you be starting up a business that deals in land, you could contact the U.S. Department of Agriculture, which has a Business and Industry Guaranteed Loan Program. Of course you can also look for state government programs. There are also plenty of green incentives, such as the EPS's SmartWay Transport Partnership, which provides funding to trucking companies that are doing what they can through alternative means or technology, to save fuel, and minimize pollution. Consider your business and your industry, and determine which branch of the federal or local government might be inclined to support your efforts. If you are especially innovative and have created some new type of technology that generates significant attention, you can apply for a Small Business Innovation Research (SBIR) program award. They provide $1.1 billion in funding to small businesses on the cutting edge of technology. While it's not easy to attain, if you're tech savvy, you might find the backing you need from the SBIR.

In addition, a number of states have financing programs, some of which are designed to support job growth. Rhode Island, for example, has had a program called Job Bank, which will provide loans to qualifying companies that can provide a certain number of jobs. Local small business development centers might be able to help you find funding.

The EPA can also help you find green building programs in your state, such as the Energy Efficiency Financing Program from the California Energy Commission, or the Renewable Energy Trust, which is part of the Massachusetts Technology Collaborative. You'll find other green building programs at the EPA website (epa.gov).

Also check with trade unions in your industry. Often they can direct you to potential sources of funding.

# Other Options

Yes, there are venture capitalists, typically looking to provide capital for startup or expansion to a hot up-and-coming business from which they can see returns of 25 percent and up in the not-too-distant future. Unlike an angel investor, however, a venture capitalist manages a fund and is looking for suitable investments for that fund. An angel investor is an individual who, while also looking for a suitable investment, is looking for a personal opportunity. Venture capitalists, on the other hand, will likely have no business experience in your industry, but are focused, more like a bank, on rate of return. Unlike a bank, you can get money quickly from a venture capitalist; however, as noted above they are looking for a high rate of return on their investment while a bank is looking only for you to pay back your loan on time, with interest.

There are a host of green venture capitalists that look to finance businesses involved in renewable energy, clean air technologies, clean water technologies, and so on. In fact, the number of "green" venture-backed businesses has risen sharply in recent years from only 74 in 2005—involving roughly $600 million dollars—to nearly 225 in 2007 at a value of $3 billion dollars. One place to explore such green VCs is the Eco Businesslinks website at: ecobusinesslinks.com/green_venture_capital.htm.

> **Smart Tip**
> According to the White House the average SBA loan size is $152,000 and the average for microloans is $13,000.

# Financing on Your Own

For those of you who have saved up with a business in mind, you can start off with your own little nest egg. Many small-business owners have set aside bonus checks or income from outside sources (like the $10,000 you won at the track) to become entrepreneurs. Often, such personal savings along with a small unsecured bank loan can be enough to get the business off the ground. Unsecured loans are much easier to obtain than business loans, assuming you have a good credit rating and a record of paying off debts.

It's ill-advised to put your house up as collateral on a home equity loan to start a business since, despite your plans, a business idea can fail and you don't want to risk your home. You can sell off other assets to raise money or, should you be a retiree rattling around in a large home, you might opt to downsize to a smaller house and use the money from the sale of your larger home to start up a business. There are many possibilities.

Personal credit cards are yet another common source of startup cash, although you have to make sure you watch your expenses very closely. You don't want to skimp on equipment and tools, but when you're paying with plastic, it can be tempting to buy equipment with all the bells and whistles when just the basics will do. There are also business lines of credit that you can take out. However, these, which work like personal credit lines, are more typically used for repairs or special projects and not for startup costs.

In the end, the bottom line is that you evaluate the various means of coming up with the green to go green. If you show that you have a solid business plan plus the enthusiasm, knowledge, and smarts to take a business idea from the drawing board to fruition, you can, with some searching, find the necessary funding. And remember, you will draw supporters and possibly even backers by being green, so let your plans for sustainability be known.

# Making Your Way in a Greener World

In this chapter we'll take a look at some of the ways in which you can work your environmental plans, goals, and ideas into your business and, while being green, can also make some green.

# Making Money

Can green businesses make money today? A resounding "yes" is the answer you will hear from a rapidly widening audience for green products and services. The growing concerns of the nation, and the world, are echoing through almost all industries and being heard loud and clear by millions of business owners and consumers. No longer are environmentalists a subcategory or niche, they are in the mainstream, whether it means living off the grid and eating organic or trying to recycle as often as possible and saving paper by printing on both sides of the page, people are taking environmental concerns more seriously than ever before.

Of course making money is about more than being green. It's about knowing what the public wants and how to price products and/or services accordingly. It's about marketing (coming up later in the book) and customer relations. In a highly industrialized society with amazing technological advances, even the most basic crafts maker needs to stay one step ahead of the learning curve when it comes to being on the edge of customer wants and needs. He or she needs to know what is coming around the bend, so to speak. Additionally, business owners must be able to find that balance between making money and staying green. "I wanted to help conserve the environment," says Thanh Yua, founder of Selfish Box, makers of gourmet lunches in Redmond, Washington, who found that the greener packaging was three times more costly than traditional packaging. "Even though green was important, making money was more important because I wanted to get the business off the ground So, I had to find the balance between the cost of being green and the ability to make money. I had to find my own lines and boundaries," explains Hua. She would go on to use her years of technology training to save money in other areas of the business by using technology to have a paperless office, control the inventory, and run the kitchen more efficiently.

Many entrepreneurs will have that same important decision to make when it comes to where money should be spent and costs need to be cut. Good entrepreneurs are those who weigh all of the factors, use their own expertise, and make the right choices. In fact, business owners who have made the wrong choices, such as cutting on product quality to spend more on advertising, have learned the hard way that you need to know where and when to save and where and when to spend. Green can be costlier in some areas, while saving you money in others. As many entrepreneurs have discovered, you need to know how to create a balance.

# Knowledge

"We initially went to natural product shows, looked at the market and tried to decide what would be a good product," says Nell Newman, of Newman's Own

Organics. "At that time the natural foods industry was a lot younger and there weren't that many really good organic food products available. It was not like today where you can get anything. Finding a manufacturer that could make a product that was willing to be certified organic (meaning properly labelled, organic foods being segregated, etc.) wasn't a necessity but we knew certification was coming so we decided that whatever plants we used should be certified organic," adds Nell, referring to the Organic Food Act of 1990, which was not implemented when Newman Organics started, but would be in the near future. This meant staying ahead of the curve and when certification was later introduced, Newman's Own Organics were already there.

Making money is largely about knowing your business inside and out. When you talk with Kelly LaPlante of Laplante Organic Interior Designs, about organic design, Nell Newman about organic foods, or the folks at Clif Bar about health bars they, like many entrepreneurs, can go on and on. It's that knowledge about their industry (and the environment) that puts them at the forefront of the green business evolution. It's been repeated many times in many industries, but there is no substitute for knowledge.

Once you know your business thoroughly, you can tell quality products from substandard, fair prices from rip-offs, and what items will make money for you from those that will not. Talk to the owner of a typical small business, especially a mom-and-pop shop owner who has been in business for 25 years, he or she can talk about every piece of merchandise in the store and tell you why it's there and who buys it. That's the first key to making money knowing your business inside and out.

# Pricing

Yes, organic still costs more than traditional and you may need to charge more for some green products largely because they are not produced in mass volume. On the other hand, you need to stay within a price range that suits the product or service and the needs of your customers. Once upon a time, products and services typically fell into a somewhat standard price range. Perhaps a sweater would be purchased for anywhere from $25 to $100 depending on the quality and the fabric. Today, however, you'll find sweaters selling for $50, $300 and $3,000. Why? Because there are markets for very discerning customers as well as the mainstream market. There are a wealth of fabrics, leading designers, and a buying market for items priced at a wider range than ever before. Sure there are common household items that fit within basic parameters and fall into standard competitive pricing, but the options, features offered, and various other details have significantly increased the possibilities.

You need to look at your market carefully and determine what customers are looking to spend on your products or services. You will need to determine carefully your costs to buy and ship products or make products from various materials and then ship them. Remember, labor costs need to be included. If, for example you are making body lotion and your sum total of costs for the product (including labor, packaging, and shipping) comes to $5 per bottle and you are selling it at $8 per bottle, you are making $3 per item or a 38 percent mark-up per bottle. If organic body lotion bumps up your cost to $4 per bottle, you can move your price up to $9 per item. If people in your demographic group are used to paying in the $6 to $10 range and are sold on the advantages of organic products (from your green marketing) then you are fitting right into that prospective price range. If, however, you are forced to pay more and need to charge $13 per bottle, you might price yourself out of the comfortable and familiar price range of your customers.

Pricing is about:

1. What customers expect to pay
2. What you need to spend to purchase products, or on the materials to make products
3. What you can afford to charge
4. What the competitive prices are
5. How you can justify higher prices if necessary.

The old notion of supply and demand will also work its way into the equation at some point. If you are the only business in an area selling organic wine then you can charge a little more. If there are three other stores selling organic wine, you will have to stay very close to their prices or justify why your prices are higher. If you are charging a dollar more and donating that dollar to a wildlife fund, you may do fine with green-minded customers. If you are charging a dollar more and have no justifiable reason, you may lose customers to your competition.

It's intriguing that today many businesses are on the cutting edge of environmental products. Therefore, as they ponder what move to make next, you can step in and grab a market share with a truly well-presented, well-marketed greener version of a product, which is exactly how GreeNow, the company that started renting out biodiesel generators and forklifts for events, movie shoots, and construction jobs, got their green edge on the competition. In addition, pricing was certainly in their favor.

"With the rising price of gasoline, biodiesel has become a more cost-effective option," says Aaron Levinthal, co-owner of GreeNow.

Today, pricing is also about customer trust, comfort, and personal service. Personalized service may not show up on expense reports, but it is a money maker, especially in an environmentally conscious world where "back to the basics" means back to interacting with other people. The faceless companies and faceless department stores are once again giving way to personalized, low-tech communication. Yes, you

## Shortcut to Better Pricing

**Y**ou can use the following three-step guideline to make pricing products a little easier:

- ○ *Consider your production costs.* This not only includes the materials, but the labor, salaries of your workers, rent, and everything else you need to spend to stay in business.
- ○ *Review the market.* Look at the buying market (your customers) and do some research to determine what they are willing to pay. Also look at the prices your competitors are charging. Then see what makes your product or service different.
- ○ *Set guidelines.* Determine the absolute minimum you can charge for a product or service without losing money and the absolute high you could charge that would still be reasonable. Then look to set a price somewhere in between depending on how in-demand your product or service is at the moment—you can always have sales and lower prices or raise them slightly if you don't think you will lose your customers.

can charge a little more because of the "hello" factor, meaning you are actually greeting customers and interacting with them. Even if you are running an online business, you can use the interactive capabilities of the internet to stay in touch with your customers through specialized e-mailings, discussion boards, online newsletters, questions and answers, blogs, and by being transparent. Personalized attention can merit slightly higher pricing and typically costs you little or nothing.

You can also do as Clif Bar does and make your commitment to the environment very clear and highly visible. Note your green initiatives or community involvement and activities on your website, in your promotional materials, and in your newsletter.

# Inventory

In the retail world, you need inventory to survive, or so they say. Online sites ship from fulfillment houses and many businesses send directly from the factories with whom they have distribution agreements. Even actual bricks-and-mortar stores are finding ways of curtailing inventory to save on money and the emissions created by ongoing shipments being trucked back and forth. Several smaller stores offer customers kiosks and other means of viewing additional products that they may not have on hand but can ship directly to the customer's home. This allows for making the sale while not having to stock a huge inventory. It combines the catalog and web sales concepts with the retail store, where the most popular products can be featured. You may notice some of the popular sneaker outlets, among other stores, have smaller yet successful locations in the malls. They pay lower rent, spend less on energy costs, and still sell products at the same rate. In short, you can find ways to minimize inventory and space and still maximize profits while doing less damage to the environment. It's a win-win situation.

> **Smart Tip** *Tip...*
>
> If you are storing inventory in your home, seek out the optimal location depending on the needs of the product. While clothing is fairly easy to store, items that are heat or cold sensitive must be in areas in which you can adjust the temperature if necessary. Also look for dry locations. Portions of inventories have been lost in basements that flood. Know your home and where your merchandise will be best kept safely.

As for your "green" inventory, only you can judge how well your client base will respond to green choices. You might elect to carry all organic products, or, like The Green Office and many other businesses, offer green choices wherever possible but maintain customers by meeting their needs with traditional products as well. This keeps customers coming back and at least some of their purchases are of the greener variety. As is the case with many businesses today, you can donate to 1% for the Planet or another worthy green association—there are many reputable ones from which to choose so do some research. In some cases, inventory simply means utilizing the space you have carefully. Jennifer Doob, who runs her homebased business, Wild Dill, selling a wealth of organic products for kids, has her inventory on hand. "I buy a lot from local Bay Area manufacturers and keep my inventory in my home," explains Doob, referring to her garage and attic that are filled with products. "It's been a challenge, but so far it works. I also try to ship in boxes that have some recycled content and use recycled paper and packing peanuts made from corn," adds Jennifer.

# Ordering from Green Suppliers

WalMart made a point of letting suppliers know that they were instituting a scorecard, so to speak, to determine who was green and who was not. In essence, this was their way of selecting to work with green suppliers. Depending on your industry, you, too, can opt to work with greener businesses by reviewing the business practices of your potential suppliers. No, they may not be 100 percent green, but if you see that they are using renewable energy and/or recycling and reusing older products, you can determine that the supplier is of the same mindset as yourself. Look at other factors when making up your criteria, including packaging and modes of shipping. Are you getting tons of Styrofoam packing peanuts or are items shipped with recyclable newspaper or organic packing peanuts? If you review the various areas in which suppliers could be greener and set up a list of criteria, you can then select those who meet at least some of your criteria. This could include the use of:

- organic products
- recyclable materials
- nontoxic predicts and processes
- means of packaging
- means of shipping.
- waste of excess product materials
- waste of excess packaging materials

and more.

You can also work with local manufacturers and cut down on the shipping and subsequent carbon emissions. In addition, you are supporting your local market.

# Manufacturing Environmentally-Friendly Products

From baking to making toys, clothing, or other products, if you are in any type of manufacturing business, you will want to think green, organic, and sustainable to stay in step with the times. In fact, in many industries, stricter regulations are now in place to make sure you tow the line. However, there is always more you can do.

It is, therefore, up to ownership and management to launch topdown initiatives that motivate research and development teams to make environmentally friendlier products high on the priority list. In a very small operation, you are the top, middle, and lower management. The trick is to evaluate the products you make and determine whether there are organic, natural, or greener alternatives that will not sacrifice the quality. Until recent years, for example, most organic food products were high on natural ingredients and low in taste. Today, however, as evidenced by Newman's Own Organics and Clif Bar, the quality of food is at the same level, or higher, than your "less" healthy alternatives. Likewise, organic cotton has made an impact in the clothing industry and lightweight, sleeker LCD computer screens have taken over from the energy-burning CRTs to the delight of their users. Yes, energy efficient and natural can be welcomed with open arms, as long as you meet the same standards that an energy and non-organic society has gotten used to.

"The question you want to ask yourself is: How close are my products to nature?" notes environmental journalist Trish Riley, author of *The Complete Idiot's Guide to Green Living*. As she points out, you want to determine how sustainable your products are going to be, meaning that if they are made with synthetic chemicals, you are not yet there.

Energy-efficient appliances, earth-friendly cleaning products, organic wines and beers, and clothing made from bamboo are all evidence that whatever you are making, there is a greener alternative. Bio-plastics are now more readily available than ever before and recyclable plastics made from corn starch, pea starch, and vegetable oil are all making headway in the manufacturing of numerous products. Check out bio-plastics magazine (bioplasticsmagazine.com) for more on the evolution of plastics in the new eco-friendly world.

Then there is Teko Socks, a Colorado-based company that makes socks from organic cotton, wool from a family farm in Tasmania, and/or recycled polyester made from old soda bottles and industrial waste. And if it's French pastries you crave, how about some organic ones from Miette, a small completely organic pasteria in the eco-friendly Ferry Building in San Francisco. People in a very wide range of industries are taking a new perspective on common products, evaluating what functions need to be served, and then determining if there is an alternative way of making them that is organic or recyclable. If not, is there a way of reusing the product? Ingenuity is very much appreciated when it comes to new uses for old products.

Along with creating and using earth-friendly products, materials, and/or ingredients, you'll want to keep chemicals out of the manufacturing process. From the building industry to the print industry, toxins and chemicals used in the manufacturing process are major contributors to air and water pollution.

# Growing It Yourself

While manufacturers can create their own greener products and materials, businesses in the food and beverage industry can grow some of their own ingredients, cutting down on costs,

## Dollar Stretcher

If you're in the food business, take a cue from Zabars in New York City or Ubuntu, a stylish upscale vegetable restaurant in Napa, California, and grow some of it yourself. Homegrown fresh vegetables and herbs and spices can save you thosands of dollars annually. Many chefs today, when not in the kitchen, are spending time in the garden.

while making sure that the ingredients are natural. "We grow our own herbs," says Thanh Hua, of gourmet lunch makers Selfish Box. Hua estimates that the business saves $30 a week just on basil. Many businesses have added their own gardens, which cuts down on shipping and assures freshness. The well-known Eli Zabar's grocery store and restaurant on the upper west side of Manhattan is a prime example of using urban rooftop space for agriculture. Upon the sprawling roof, you'll find commercial-size production greenhouses with raised beds filled with greens, herbs, and tomatoes. This is the urban answer to growing and selling your own produce, much as farmers do with their own farm stands. Even businesses that do not cater to the palate have embarked on the trend of growing natural foods. For example, Pangea Organics, makers of organic skin care products, have a garden where workers plant and grow their own foods for their fellow employees to enjoy. The land is given by the company for the express purpose of farming—talk about sustainability!

# Sustainable Packaging and Packing

Packaging today is designed to be easily disposable, which means "let's just toss it," to most people. Unfortunately more than half of that packaging (40 million tons annually) gets tossed rather than recycled, and ends up in landfill, in our oceans and water-ways, or your nearby city dump. Sustainable packaging minimizes energy as well as the disposable effects of packaging. The idea is to use packaging that has a closed loop, or a cyclical lifecycle, going from nature back to nature. Materials used for sustainable packaging need to be biodegradable, made from recyclable and reusable materials and created through eco-friendly methods. Using recycled materials presents an opportunity to recover valuable raw materials, thereby allowing you to create economic value by eliminating the basic extraction and processing steps.

Before launching a business, an entrepreneur can review exactly where packaging material will come from and what types of materials can be used to create such a recyclable and sustainable lifecycle. From a product standpoint, you will need to determine the type of packaging that will keep products fresh and safe during shipping or during a shelf life. You will then need to see if you can create such eco-friendly alternatives that will meet those needs and/or eliminate energy waste in the process. Some possibilities are more practical than others, depending on the product(s) in question. For example, you may be able to utilize biodegradable plastics, rather than those that are petroleum based. Other solutions may include using materials with recyclable natural fibers or corrugated cardboard. You'll want to look at packaging as it goes from your company as a manufacturer all the way to the end consumer.

For Curtis Packaging, a 163-year-old luxury packaging company based in Sandy Hook, Connecticut, the move to sustainability became a conscious initiative. "About five years ago we decided to look at trying to green the business and be more environmentally friendly, as well as remaining luxurious, so we dubbed ourselves 'luxuriously responsible,'" explains Don Droppo, Jr., Vice President for Sales and Marketing.

Today, some five years later, Curtis has made a major commitment to renewable energy and now has a 100 percent carbon neutral footprint. But it was not just in their operations that they made an impact. "In luxury packaging, people use foils, and that's not recyclable, so we came out with a new product called Curt Chrome, which is an environmentally friendly alternative to foil. It's metallic-based ink and 100 percent recyclable," explains Droppo of one of the many environmentally sound products now available from Curtis.

It is this type of eco-friendly packaging that other companies have also taken into consideration. Even a giant company, Procter & Gamble, for example, has introduced new rigid tubes for Crest toothpaste that can be shipped and displayed on shelves without boxes. Another, company, Aveda, makers of beauty products, uses bottles made from 95 percent recycled materials, while beauty giant Estee Lauder created a new tube design that comes from 80 percent recycled aluminum.

Along with packaging, you can also move to greener packing materials in an effort to replace some of the landfill favorites such as Styrofoam peanuts. First, consider that most packages have an overabundance of packing materials and simply by limiting such excess you can be more eco-friendly. Today, there are biodegradable packing peanuts available, made from grain sorghum and corn starch. Besides being 100 percent biodegradable, they are static free and not affected by oil prices. There are various brands available including Puffy Stuff, which is quite durable and cost effective (see puffystufftn.com). Soft foam, sold in rolls, is also made from corn starch and soybean oils. Then there are real peanuts or, at least, peanut shells. And don't forget pea straw which can actually be replanted by whomever receives your packages. Shredded thin wood shavings, known as excelsior, are also good natural packing materials, as are shredded newspapers or shredded cardboard boxes. You can also use rolled up (non-shredded) newspapers placed into the packaging around the content.

The point is, packaging materials can be both eco friendly and cost efficient. You need only to take the time to think through both packaging and packing as you build and create your business. "Think about each step of the process," says Dan Kennedy, owner and creative force behind Long Island-based chocolate makers, Chokola'j. In fact, Kennedy not only utilizes recyclable packaging but recommends ways to reuse the packaging on the company's website (chokolajchocolate.com) such as using the linen-embossed chocolate boxes to save recipes or note cards.

# Greener Shipping

Hybrid cars and trucks, the use of biodiesel, and local suppliers are among the ways in which shipping can be greener. Additionally, following Clif Bar's lead and making sure your distributors are close to your retail locations can help cut down on carbon emissions. Chokola'j buys as much as possible locally to limit the need for shipping and thus reduces fossil fuel expenditures. They also buy ingredients directly from local growers and farms to cut out the need to ship first to distributors and then to the company.

Other recommendations include shipping small items by bike messenger rather than using a van to take a folder or small package across town. You should also make sure your vehicles have fully inflated tires, which saves on fuel. In many instances, you can avoid shipping completely by using electronic means of distribution rather than printing catalogs, reports, or long texts and shipping them all over the place. "We use an online catalog to cut down on the need for printing and shipping," explains Dan Kennedy of Chokola'j, adding that it is also a cost savings, which allows for spending a little more money for organic products.

Along with recycling packaging and reusing packing materials, another, less talked about means of greener shipping is to recycle pallets. Shipping pallets, also known as skids, are the flat wood structures that keep products and materials stable when being loaded by a forklift or similar type of device. Actually, they can also be made of plastic or metal. "We take part in a pallet recycling program," notes Dan Garrido of the Washington-based Inu Treats.

Since wood is an environmentally sustainable product that is easily recyclable and reusable, the most common pallets are made from wood and can be utilized and reused frequently through a well-managed pallet recovery and reuse program. Under their Rediscovered Wood Certification Program, the Rain Forest Alliance Smart Wood Program, uses a GP logo on the pallets as certification. Essentially, this program keeps the pallets in use. For more on the recycling of pallets, visit smartwood.com and type in "pallets" to find their pallets recovery program.

# Greener Service with a Smile

To this point, the focus has been primarily on retail and manufacturing businesses. Service-based businesses can also start and maintain a green mandate. The key is in how you perform the service that you are selling. If you are teaching dance, karate, or aerobics, are you using a facility that uses some natural means of heating, cooling, and lighting or an HVAC system that utilizes a lot of energy? If you are detailing cars, operating a cleaning service, or painting homes, are you using nontoxic chemicals and/or paints? If you are catering, are you using hybrid vehicles and organic foods? The point is, the tools of your trade, the office in which you work, and your means of commuting can all be potentially green. Some service providers are finding that they can utilize the web to offer uploads and downloads as alternative ways to provide information. From webinars to online instruction, services that might have once meant energy spent on transportation and wasted paper or other goods can now be in the hands of clients or customers via the internet. You can even adopt paperless billing practices as you look for ways to green your service-based business.

# Greener Commuting

Ridespring (ridespring.com) helps businesses with car pool scheduling and also encourages alternative means of transportation (to driving) by giving away prizes. You can also consider means by which you can encourage employees, and even customers, to opt for a bike, a car pool (or van pool), or a brisk walk to your facility rather than driving. Don't forget there's also mass transit as an option. While it's not green unto itself, 25 people on a bus means 25 fewer people driving individually to work.

Many businesses encourage biking to work, while other companies even pick up all or part of the tab for mass transit. For those who might prefer carpooling, if only they didn't feel lost without accessibility to a car during the day, you can consider Zipcar (zipcar.com) as a means of having cars on hand for employees who need them. The two companies, each provide innovative means of having a car available when necessary. Unlike a rental car, which is costly and needs to be picked up at a specific location, a Zip car is a low-emission or hybrid vehicle parked near a work location. Your employees, can have a card as access to the vehicle for use when necessary. You can outline how this system of determine what is and is not "necessary" will work. Your company then pays Zipcar an hourly rate that includes gas, insurance, and

## Smart Tip

Did you know that in Amsterdam, 33 percent of all trips are made by bicycle? In Copenhagen, 33 percent of all commuters use bicycles to get to and from work. In the United States, however, where more than 100 million Americans (or nearly 33 percent of the world's population) own bicycles, it is estimated that about 1 percent bike to and from work. The potential for alternative commuting is there, but incentives need to be provided to get people out of their vehicles and onto those bicycles.

maintenance. It's far less expensive than owning and operating a car, and much more convenient than renting.

While you cannot make people use alternative means of transportation, you can certainly provide rewards, such as hours off, free lunch, or other perks for those who excel in finding alternative ways of commuting.

# Teaming with Likeminded Companies

Small businesses today do not have to go it alone. Along with the Small Business Administration, many entrepreneurs find local chambers of commerce and business or civic-minded associations very helpful. Even cooperatives, linking several businesses together to buy in mass quantity as well as share resources, can benefit the entrepreneur. In the green business environment, entrepreneurs with likeminded goals and similar environmental concerns can team up to create community initiatives or take action and make a difference on specific projects. Non-competitive businesses can benefit one another in various ways, including the use of office space, shared advertising costs, and even shared shipping if the companies are close to one another. Why not double up that which is being shipped in one truck rather than have two separate half full trucks taking a similar route?

There are plenty of worthwhile environmental causes that can bring businesses together. Explore those in your area. Several merchants, for example, might start recycling programs for computer cartridges or other specific items that can be brought in by customers. Perhaps you can initiate and sponsor a farmer's market selling locally grown produce. There are plenty of possibilities.

# People Power

## Your Green Team and Your Community

There are a few key groups of people that make up a successful business. In this chapter we will discuss two of them, your employees (who we're calling your "green team") and your community, which is made up of those in the geographic area around your business and in the industry in which you are a part. Two other groups are your suppliers, whom we discussed briefly earlier, and your customers (probably the most significant group since without them you have no business). We will return to customers in the next chapter when we discuss marketing, promotion, and advertising, since that is how you will reach them.

Starting a new business gives you an opportunity to surround yourself with like-minded people. Since most small businesses start out with only a few employees, and sometimes they are primarily freelancers or part timers, you can discuss your vision for an environmentally-friendly business and see if they nod in agreement, flinch, or look at you as if you have two heads. Today, it's very likely that your hiring pool of possible employees will have a fair number of green-minded candidates. However, while this can be a plus, you still want to balance the equation with good people who know how to put in a full day's work. The ongoing advances in technology has created a dichotomy whereby you will find people who thrive on high-tech tools and can accomplish an amazing amount of tasks in a shorter time than ever before. Conversely, you will find those who use technology to take short cuts or as a means of "looking busy." Your goal is to weed out the doers from the posers.

Hiring employees means not only looking at resumes and credentials but actually checking those references and even using online background checking services if necessary to make sure someone really is who they say they are and has done what they say they have. It is advantageous to have a pre-application form available to gather a lot of basic data before interviewing and hiring people. Review an application with your attorney before handing it out since, by law, you cannot ask certain questions. For example you can ask if someone is over the age of 18, but not someone's exact age. You also need to be careful when interviewing people to avoid personal questions and to stick to the subject at hand: working for your company.

Assessing the personality and professionalism of any prospective employee is not always easy. It is, however, important. The individual's traits and ability to interact with others can help you bring on board quality personnel at any level. Environmental concerns, as discussed by a candidate, can indicate a level of thinking beyond the common "me" syndrome that is also so pervasive today. Of course you need to determine whether or not someone is genuine or greenwashing you. You can get a general idea by bringing up sustainability and environmental concerns (at a basic level) during an interview.

It is also advantageous to have a printed or electronic employee manual in advance. This

**Smart Tip**

*Tip...*

When you interview candidates, don't wing it. It's to your advantage to have some questions and/or topics at the ready on a list before you start your interview. This way you don't go off on tangents and end up discussing only the enivoment while not learning about the work history and skills of the individual.

allows you to cover the ways in which you want employees to carry themselves when they work in your company. Within such a manual you will want to include subjects such as:

- tardiness
- vacations
- personal and/or sick days
- any benefits you offer
- policies regarding theft, drug or alcohol use, sexual harassment, etc. (have an attorney look over this part to make sure you do not open yourself up to any liability)
- security
- parking
- use of office or company facilities, etc.
- grounds for termination

You can include whatever you like, which also means that perks, bonuses, or any other incentives can also be part of your policies. Clif Bar, among other companies, allows for a few days off each year, with pay, to do volunteer work. "We called it the 2080 Program, since that's the number of hours people typically work in a year," explains Kate Torgerson, head of Clif Bar Public Relations. Employees may volunteer with pay for several hours per week. Clif Bar and other businesses also have company-wide employee initiatives, such as cleaning up a local beach or park. This, too, is counted as part of the employee's regular hours if he or she participates.

Some companies offer incentives, whether sales based, green based, or simply for perfect attendance. As a perk, New Belgium Brewery gives each employee a bicycle after one year of employment. Whatever you choose to do in terms of green incentives can be part of your employee manual. You will then want to have each employee sign that they have read the material and save their signatures. This way, you can claim that you had the regulations and policies in print and the employee read them, in the event that there is ever a dispute between employees and management.

# Establishing a Green Business Culture

Of course before you can hire people, you'll need to know specifically what you are looking for. This means not only defining specific positions within your business, but also having an idea of your business as a whole. If you want your staff to fit into your company's culture, you will have to define that culture in advance. This means evaluating, or re-evaluating, your beliefs, particularly your environmental concerns.

You might want to write down your idea of what the company's culture should be so that you can more closely match likeminded employees to your company vision. This way you will be better able to attract the kind of people that will be most comfortable working for your business. In some cases, you will find people with the knowledge and skills that not only fit your business but also cross over into environmental concerns. In other cases, you will find individuals with more passion than knowledge and experience. Sometimes taking raw resources and shaping them, as in the case of training bright and ambitious newcomers, can be very rewarding. There are many people today who are anxious to make an impact on the environment but need some lessons in exactly how they can do so. This may be your opportunity to impart your knowledge upon the next green generation.

As you build a staff with whom you feel comfortable, you will also build an image that draws in shareholders, stakeholders, and customers and that fits comfortably within your business culture. Remember, most businesses present a personality of sorts, or an image, that transcends the place of business and includes the products, reputation, and service provided.

You'll find many job candidates sporting impressive credentials with degrees or diplomas from excellent universities. However, in many cases the green component of their job will be added later, through your training. Today, we are all learning greener methods of doing many jobs and positions like "sustainability director" are evolving as we all continue around an environmental learning curve that is expanding. Almost every day, there are new breakthroughs regarding environmentally safer, cleaner, or energy-efficient ways of doing jobs and making a difference. In some cases, they are actually old ways of doing things that are being revitalized with new vigor and passion. Either way, there is steady news evolving on the environmental front every day.

## I Now Pronounce You Business Partners

There are many husband-and-wife teams starting up businesses today, as evidenced by our list of 22 green businesses back in Chapter 2. Most of these couples share the idea of creating a sustainable business. It is, however, important whenever teaming with someone—spouse, or not—to recognize each other's strengths and weaknesses. This will allow you to determine who best fits which role. For example, Daniel Kennedy of Chokola'j, the organic candymakers, takes the lead when it comes to the creative side, using his years of experience as a chef, while his wife Susan uses her business know-how to handle the business side.

Keep in mind that it is easy to post the word "green" on your business and on your website, but you'll be much further ahead if you plant and nurture a green culture within your workforce from the start. So, take the time to evaluate what your business culture will be.

# A Green Team

While we are using the term "green team" as a means of simply defining employees of a green business, some businesses, as they get larger, actually put together a specific green team to assess the manner in which the business is being run and review possible ways of being greener. Such teams are usually the result of volunteers stepping forward. With support and guidance by management and ownership (that's you), a green team can research and report on various means of improving sustainability within a company.

A successful green team taps into the areas of expertise of the various individuals. For example, someone who heads up production, facilities, or management might look into waste management alternatives, while your shipping department can research and present alternative shipping methods and your marketing department can consider greener means of marketing. In nearly every business someone (typically the office manager) is in charge of office supplies, so he or she could be setting up a greener purchasing policy for such supplies.

In a small business, two or three people can wear various hats. "I had to learn about marketing, promotion, shipping, and handle all areas of a business," explains Jennifer Doob, of Wild Dill. Likewise, Kelly LaPlante, of LaPlante Organic Interior Designs, also had to juggle the various areas that it takes to run a business. "I was fortunate to have a lot of good people around me including friends who were supportive and wanted to help out," says LaPlante.

Whether you have an actual "green team" or, as a very small business, you simply establish some basics for yourself and your partner to follow, you'll want to cover the environmentally significant areas including:

## Dollar Stretcher

Hire experts when necessary. While this doesn't sound like a way of saving money, it is. First, by bringing in someone with expertise to handle your bookkeeping or public relations, you are freeing up your time to focus on what you do best. In addition, the mistakes that people make trying to handle areas of business in which they have no background or experience can add up to significant losses ... plus you then need to have a professional to come in and clean up the mess. Therefore, money well spent is, in the long run, a dollar saver.

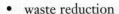
- waste reduction
- energy conservation
- water conservation
- recycling
- establishing green purchasing policies
- alternative means of transportation
- use of natural resources
- renewable energy

## Smart Tip

Tip...

Green people: "Surround yourself with people who share your ideas and your vision," says Dan Garrido of Inu Treats organic pet snacks, who hired a marketing company that shares his green mindset. While everyone you work with may not be as dedicated to the environment as you are, it is advantageous to look for printers, designers, copywriters, and even lawyers who "get it" and have a sense of what you are trying to accomplish by being a green business. "It makes it much easier if you are on the same page," adds Garrido.

Not only can working together as a green team make a significant impact on the environmental future of a company, but also it can, and often does, serve as an excellent means of team building. Employees who are dedicated to environmental issues will also feel a much stronger commitment to the company if they take on an active role.

Even in what is primarily a one-person operation, you can surround yourself with your own green team of sorts. Carolyn Deal of Sum-Bo Shine natural baby care products teams up with several likeminded individuals who help her with graphics, technology, and other areas of expertise. "I handle the operations, but I work with several people some of whom are mentors, such as a chemcial engineer who has an MBA and provides support and expertise in the field," explains Carolyn, who has connected with people who share her interest in the environment and provide various levels of help and support through their networking efforts.

# Green Protocol

The key to a green business is starting with the right mindset. If everyone in a company thinks about recycling from day one, then it becomes standard everyday practice within the company. Likewise, if everyone sets their computer on sleep mode when they are away from their desk for a short period of time and turns their computers off when leaving their desks for a longer time span, it simply becomes the way things are done. The reason we are in this global warming crisis is largely because for decades we, as a nation, have continued to engage in the same bad habits. Throughout the 20th century we found better, quicker, faster, more expedient ways of building things, of getting places, and of doing business. We dazzled ourselves with innovation after innovation without regard for the impact such energy-expending technology was having on our planet. We became a wasteful society by our own indulgence.

Today, a new business can right some of the mistakes of the past by invoking policies that take a step back. Part of the environmental mindset is the idea of going back to nature, a place where we were prior to such tremendous industrialization. This doesn't mean getting rid of technology, but simply learning how to curb our excesses. It means bringing nature back into vogue by utilizing natural resources wherever possible, such as rainwater to clean your office and water your plants.

If you set up the ways and means of doing things in a greener manner from the start, you will build eco-friendly habits. You will also have an advantage over long-standing competitors in that you will not need to take time and effort to rectify the mistakes of the past and rethink previous ways of conducting business.

# Building a Collective (or "Team") Mindset

Policies, guidelines, and protocol (green or otherwise) can put you on the right path, but only a motivated team, working together, can make a business flourish. While we will discuss the importance of social responsibility later in the book, it is at this point (discussing employees and employers) that we will begin discussing the ways in which you will build the unity that makes a company move forward together. Remember that achieving a comfortable work-life balance makes both employees and company owners happier. Therefore, here are a few suggestions that might help you build a cohesive unit from the onset. After all, why wait to boost morale when you can get it going with a jump start from the beginning.

1. *Ask for suggestions*. By listening to ideas from all sides, you bring everyone into the equation. While you can't use every suggestion, you can show appreciation for each one and explain why it might not work at present. By implementing some of the better suggestions, you let employees know that they, too, have a sense of ownership in the company, which is huge for morale.

2. *Schedule company activities*. This is where you can implement some green activities if you choose. Whether you schedule activities that are simply fun, or benefit a neighborhood or charity, it is this kind of team building that can bring people together outside of the work atmosphere. From a company picnic to a corporate retreat, such activities create a bond among people.

3. *Offer family-oriented benefits*. The trend in businesses today, large and small, is to recognize that employees do have families and that you can better motivate your employees by offering some family perks. From on-site day care for larger companies to simply providing some flex time or half days for family events,

you can score points with your employees by acknowledging their commitment to their families. You should also provide adequate time off for maternity leave or should an employee be adopting a child.

4. *Include incentives*. Who doesn't like a bonus? While you may be in no position as a new company to give out cash bonuses or bicycles after a year, you can certainly find smaller, low-cost perks for your employee of the week or month, or your top salesperson. Whatever you decide meets your criteria for rewarding someone on your staff, it is a plus to have some incentives (even a free lunch) to encourage your employees to do their best. Smaller, but meaningful incentives can prove most effective (unless you are giving something to everyone). This way the employee feels good, while you are not promoting a high level of competition that can backfire and impinge upon the desired team atmosphere.

5. *Find new settings for meetings*. While you won't be able to do this for all meetings, you can hold some of your get-togethers in places outside of the office or board room. Find a location where you can take in the great outdoors or go organic at a health-friendly restaurant. Every neighborhood has some interesting locations that can serve the purpose. If not, perhaps you'll find some in or around your facility. When Jerry Manuel took over as manager of the New York Mets, he moved their usual pre-game locker-room team meeting out onto the field and the team started winning. Look for that change of venue to keep people interested. You can also look for unique places for company parties.

# Your Community

Most businesses, with the exception of some homebased businesses, are part of the larger community in which they reside. As soon as you let it be known that you are open for business, you will generate interest from possible customers, the media, and your fellow business owners. While fitting into your neighborhood of choice means adhering to local laws and ordinances, it also means trying to establish a good reputation, even if your community is the cyber world.

Although many businesses quietly fit into their communities, you can opt from the beginning to do more. As we'll discuss further in the marketing chapter to follow, you can increase business by being an active participant in community activities and by initiating some activities of your own. New Belgium Brewery's Bike-ins, which are drive-in movies on their lawn, draw environmentally-conscious crowds. Other companies sponsor community fairs, festivals, concerts featuring local performers, sporting events, and other activites. Sponsoring or even just taking part in neighborhood picnics or street fairs are other ways in which to make your presence known within the community.

You can also team with charitable groups to sponsor neighborhood activities. For example, one of the many Clif Bar programs focused attention on the Wrapper Brigade. The program was launched in order to reduce the number of energy bar wrappers ending up in landfills and to help kids learn about the importance of recycling and reusing waste materials. The program included schools, community groups, and even individuals who earned money for charity by picking up wrappers. While the money goes to charity from Clif Bar, the actual wrappers are fused, woven together into a strong material, and used to make handbags and other products. This is one of numerous examples of working with the community to raise the level of awareness about the environment while contributing to charity.

Following the lead of a large company, smaller businesses can take on initiatives much like that of the 150-year-old Wells Fargo, where team members in various parts of the country contributed more than 12,000 volunteer hours to support environmental causes, which included cleanups of beaches and habitat-restoration projects. Other projects included learning to install solar panels on affordable homes in the San Francisco area and promoting the development of eco-friendly homes by sponsoring Build It Green's home tours in Northern California designed to support green building practices.

In every community, there are ways to support and promote green practices and policies. For example, in Washington, DC, the Acme Paper & Supply Company has teamed with the House of Representatives catering service to provide environmentally-friendly food service products. This includes biodegradable products such as cups, plates, and bowls, all made from natural substances that will biodegrade within 30 days.

Numerous companies today are looking at ways of greening their community while enjoying the publicity and name-brand recognition such environmentally positive action brings. In addition, returning to the subject of employees, you can attract a better pool of talent through your community efforts and involvement.

Some companies consider their community to be a much larger area—the nation, the continent, or beyond. Patagonia, for example, a leader in outdoor clothing and gear (known for being at the forefront of environmental activities) has launched numerous initiatives, such as Freedom to Roam, a long-term initiative, in conjunction with other companies and conservation organizations, dedicated to re-establishing migration wildways for animals between protected areas throughout North America. Since many animals rely on migration for survival, the goal of the program is to help these animals by finding, establishing, and maintaining connecting corridors and reconnecting isolated patches of wildlands in an effort to allow animals to roam, migrate, and survive in a very industrialized world.

While far-reaching efforts such as those of Patagonia and other businesses that have grown in size and earnings may be out of the reach of brand-new businesses, there are things you can do at the local level to start out on your community efforts. For example, you might:

▲

- *Get involved in local green activities.* Donate your time and even some sample products to worthy environmental activities in your area. If you can't spare the employees, or are simply a one- or two-person operation, you can always donate some of your profits to worthwhile environmental groups and/or organizations.

- *Team with other companies.* You need not go it alone. Together with a non-competing business, you can pool your staff and resources to make a greater impact on a green project or activity. Often, businesses can compliment one another by providing their own services, products, or the expertise of their staffers.

- *Launch your own initiative.* Run an event of your own for an environmental cause. This could be anything from a bike-a-thon to a cleanup to a dinner to raise money for a local cause. Clif Bar has hosted a number of benefit dinners such as one for the Community Alliance with Family Farmers (CAFF) and Good Humus Land Preservation Project, which raised $20,000.

- *Do pro bono work.* Utilize your skills and those of your staffers to do some non-profit work by donating your time to a good environmental cause. Train people with whom you work to also use the necessary skills to better the environment.

- *Provide education.* Whether you conduct neighborhood seminars or online webinars on the environment or visit schools and talk to school children about sustainability, you can make a difference with green teaching. You can also educate your fellow business owners with talks and demonstrations of what you do to create a greener eco-friendly environment. New Belgium Brewery, for example, gives tours of their facility to other business owners. One of those tours included some of the top brass from Wal-Mart.

Another example of an educational program is the Green Power Challenge developed in Bellingham, Washington. It is designed to educate local businesses on how and why to purchase green energy in their community. What started as an educational program has apparently proven to be quite successful—the EPA rated Bellingham one of the top green cities in the nation.

# The Homebased Business

Most homebased businesses are essentially one-person operations, or family run, with some freelancers or part timers helping out. It is, therefore, harder to build a green team, but very easy to implement your own green plans and policies. Some entrepreneurs work comfortably from their homes, limiting the use of excessive energy and utilizing reusable and/or recycled products whenever possible. Folake Kuye, who started WeWe Clothing from her home in early 2008 tries to maintain a green environment. "We try to be paperless and I don't use a lot of lights. In fact, we don't use heat or air conditioning very much either," says Folake, adding that her husband is a "hippie" and that they also try to eat organic as much as possible.

Along with being green, working from home means staying abreast of the local zoning laws. In some cases you may need a variance to set up your business in a residential community. Even if you are on the right side of the zoning laws, you'll want to maintain a low profile with your neighbors. The number of homebased travel agents, consultants, and other types of service providers has increased in recent years largely because of the internet and the ease of wireless communication. Business owners can sit quietly at their computers with their phones nearby and conduct business from the comfort of their own homes and no one is the wiser. The problems begin to emerge when trucks start making regular deliveries to a residence, cars start taking up the neighborhood parking spaces, and strangers are parading in and out of your home. These are red flags for neighborhood associations. They also may indicate that you, as a homebased business owner, have either outgrown your home office or selected a business that might simply not work from your living room, such as a fast food restaurant.

Only low-traffic businesses with minimal inventory (unless you have another location, such as a warehouse) will work from the home.

One of the biggest plusses of a homebased business is that you can eliminate commuting, and use alternative means when you have to go out to a meeting or an appointment. And you can be as green as you like, saving money on energy by opening windows and utilizing older furniture and equipment in innovative new ways.

From a business perspective, one of the hardest aspects of running a business from home is sticking to your business and not getting sidetracked. With that in mind, here are some basic home business tips:

- Make sure you establish an area of the house as your office, whether it is a dedicated space or part of a larger space. Look for an area with minimal distractions.
- Make sure you have good lighting and a comfortable workspace from which to run your business. You can use CRT light bulbs for saving energy.
- Set up your workspace so that it is optimal for accomplishing what you need to accomplish. An advantage of being homebased is that you can set everything up as you wish.
- Set up a dedicated line as a business phone so you don't have your kids' friends calling while you're in the middle of doing business.
- If you will be seeing clients or customers, set up your business in such a way that you have access to a side or back door (or can enter directly into your

workspace through the front door). The point is that you don't want everyone traipsing through your entire house.

- Have your business licenses in place and all of the necessary papers filed with your local business office. Working from a home office does not make you any less of a real, legit business, which also means Uncle Sam will be watching you.

- Find ways to keep yourself motivated and working. Set up a schedule and/or a To Do list and stick with it. Don't let yourself get into bad habits because you are not in an office building, office park, or retail location.

Homebased businesses are on the rise. If you find you are outgrowing your space you can always seek out office space. Until then, you can thrive if you are well-organized and self-motivated.

# Spreading the Word: Marketing, Promotion, and Advertising

It doesn't matter what type of business you are in ... if people don't know about you, you're not going to make money, plain and simple. In this chapter we will discuss some of the basics of marketing a small business and explore ways in which you can try to stay on the green side of marketing and promotion. Being a green business, you already have an advantage in that you are marketing yourself to a very receptive, environmentally conscious audience.

To benefit from marketing, you will want to go back to all of the market research that you have done in your efforts to zero in on a specific demographic group, or groups, that will be most receptive to your message. You can refer back to Chapter 3, Customers and Market Research, for more on the subject. Since marketing, promotion, and especially advertising, have a cost involved, as a small business owner, your job will be to look at your budget carefully and determine where you can get the most bang for your buck.

Marketing is a broad based term that covers all manners of reaching out to the public, which is why people often make up a marketing plan. This includes your product, service, pricing, projected audience or target demographic group, and how it all fits together. It is the plan that you make, based on your research, to form a brand, an image, build an identity, and reach out to your buying audience. Marketing is driven by data and research from the recent past but focuses on your future. Your analysis of the industry, the competition, pricing, buyers, and so on will reveal the key components to the

**Beware!**
There are many marketing consultants and experts out there who will, for a fee (sometimes a large one), help you put together your marketing plan. Before hiring anyone, make sure you have your own clear ideas of how you best want to present your business. Otherwise, you may be paying for a marketing plan that is all wrong. Also, consider that many small business owners have marketed themselves in the early years without any hired help. They may be asking opinions of others, exploring marketing websites, looking into SCORE, or finding mentors along the way, then, perhaps bringing in someone to hone the details once a direction has been set. Make sure whomever you bring in listens carefully to what you want.

overall picture, and like a puzzle these will make up your marketing efforts.

Effective marketing means reaching the right crowd, not necessarily the biggest crowd. It also means reaching your target audience through the papers they read, websites they visit, radio stations they listen to, TV shows they watch, and so on. Reaching 50,000 potentially strong prospects to buy your goods or services is better than reaching 500,000 people in a general audience, of which only 1 in 50, or 10,000 people are going to be interested in your products or services.

# Marketing Stories: The Good

The key is to know how to spend money wisely in an effort to effectively market your business. While most businesses will not reach the global impact of Starbucks, the Seattle-based coffee empire was originally a small business, like yours. Today, roughly 40 million customers drink Starbucks coffee every day. The Starbucks story of amazing growth has been chronicled as one of the greatest small business concept stories ever.

Chairman and CEO Howard Schultz envisioned the mass commercialization of coffee, not just as a drink but also as a lifestyle. Starbucks became known as a place where people could meet, relax, and hang out, all while having a $5 cup of exclusive coffee. Starbucks marketed what was eventually known as the "Starbucks Experience" and became a leader in the industry by using such marketing strategies and opening numerous small stores in specified areas, where people would want to take a break from the mall experience, the busy work routine, or needed a place to sit while waiting for a flight or train.

Starbucks utilized more than just a great product, they sold a lifestyle. Along with great products or services, something else is typically at the root of any major success story. In some cases, other factors are even more compelling than the product itself. MacDonald's, for example (perhaps not the *greenest* example), doesn't sell the best hamburgers in the world. Sure, they are tasty, but many steakhouses typically sell a higher quality of meat. Nonetheless, the concept of buying food quickly, at low cost, and in a kid-friendly atmosphere has made MacDonald's a household name on several continents. Like many mega success stories, it's all about marketing.

There are plenty of other great success stories built, largely, by well planned and executed marketing efforts. Take, for example, the Ronko and Popeil Brothers companies that made millions of dollars with late-night television ads for products like the Pocket Fisherman and the Veg-o-Matic in the 1970s and early 80s, before eventually going out of business because of mismanagement and a tarnished reputation at the hands of comics and television sketches. Prior to their demise, however, the founders of these two companies (father and son) made millions of dollars through marketing that focused on late-night, low-budget but highly effective television commercials. Where do you think the term "As seen on TV" came from? Their clever marketing and "buy now" ideology made impulse buying part of the American television

> **Tip...**
>
> ## Smart Tip
> Figure out what would enhance the experience of buying your product or services. Would parents buy more baby clothes if they could bring baby with them and have a sing-along? Would kids come to your dental office if the waiting room was set up as a play area? Think about what can enhance the sales experience for your buyers. If you are manufacturing, think about what would make wholesalers and store owners buy from you first. Favorable return policies? Same-day delivery? Always try to focus on one step beyond what would be considered "typical."

landscape that would later emerge on the shopping channels and those many infomercials that you see today.

# And the Bad

Of course along with the many marketing success stories come those businesses that did not fare very well. Pets.com is one of the examples that comes immediately to mind. It is infamous among the marketing world. The online website which launched in 1998 sold all sorts of pet products to consumers via the internet. Featuring what became a very well-known sock puppet, Pets.com spent a fortune blitzing the media with TV, print, and radio campaigns in 1999 and even went out to spent $1.2 million on a Super Bowl commercial in 2000. During this time, the sock puppet generated more attention than the business. The real problem was that the dot.com bubble burst and the company, hoping to make back this vast amount of money spent on marketing in four of five years of sales, could no longer get financial backing. They ran out of money very quickly because of their overzealous marketing and advertising campaigns. Meanwhile, other competing online pet supply web businesses used more carefully planned and budgeted marketing campaigns, through online newsletters and local low-budget commercials and advertisements. In time they became part of the vast retail internet landscape while Pets.com disappeared. The marketing lesson learned from Pets.com, was, as discussed earlier, that for a new company, it is more advantageous to spend less money on smaller targeted marketing efforts than it is to blow $1.2 million trying to reach everyone once with a Super Bowl ad.

# Green Marketing

While on the surface it seems easy to define green marketing, there are actually several components that can be part of the overall definition. Typically, you'll find green marketing defined as: *the marketing of products that are considered to be safer for the environment.* Of course green marketing is more than products, but includes packaging, the production process, shipping, and so on. In addition, green marketing is also about the means of marketing. For example, an organic product advertised on high-gloss paper or sold in Styrofoam packaging is defeating the purpose. Green marketing can also be used to mean; *the way in which you actually market your business*, such as on recyclable paper with soy ink, electronically to save paper, and/or by word of mouth. Finally, another definition of green marketing is: *the act of marketing to a green-minded consumer or consumer/target group.* Of course before you can market to this eco-savvy market, understand that green watchdog groups are quick to jump on greenwashers and strongly suggest that they change their ways.

Daniel Kennedy of Chokola'j, recommends starting your marketing efforts in a small, bootstrap manner. "Any time you start a new company, there's always something that doesn't come out the way you want it to. If you start small, you'll make small mistakes instead of big ones," says Kennedy, who used mostly word-of-mouth, viral marketing alignment with other businesses that shared their core values when starting up his tasty business.

For Carolyn Deal, whose passion for children, healthcare, and the environment led her to launch the Atlanta-based Sum-Bo-Shine natural baby care products, starting off small meant going to AmericasMart, Atlanta, Georgia. This combination trade show/market featured a combination of home accents, home furnishings, and personal and family products for retail buyers and wholesalers. From there it was off to other such shows, such as the Natural Exposé in Boston, where she could sell her goods to various store owners as well as to customers passing by. This relatively inexpensive means of marketing has led to Sum-Bo-Shine products now being found in stores throughout 12 states.

Dr. Stink, also known as Barry Reifman, owner of Odorzout, the all-natural, environmental way to get rid of odors, is also a fan of going to shows to promote products and look for distribution deals. "I go to different types of shows. For instance, I'll be featured in the luxury pet shows, in the green sections," explains Reifman. "There are shows in every industry, you just need to do some hunting and you can find them. I use the Dr. Stink character and wear a lab coat to stand out in the crowd. At the end of the show, people won't remember meeting Barry, but they will remember meeting Dr. Stink. It's all about making an impression," says Reifman.

David Anderson, founder and publisher of Green Options, points out that since "green" itself is not a demographic, you need to look for what it is your market wants and then think green in terms of that market. "You really just have to find the psychological or the sociological things . . . the little triggers that people don't necessarily think about all the time," explains Anderson. The point being that it's much harder to sell people on a broad, global term such as "green" or "global warming" than it is to appeal to them specifically by focusing on what they are looking for from a product or service. Sure people want to think green or learn about global warming, but it is a large, vague concept. In other words, the greenest car in the world basically means nothing to someone who doesn't drive or has no interest in buying a new car. However, if that person is looking to buy a car, he or she is far more interested in cleaner engines, biodiesel, and hybrid cars.

Of course green marketing follows the "do as I do" philosophy, meaning you need to be genuine and back up your green marketing efforts. After all, if you are claiming to be environmentally conscious in your marketing, your actions need to back your words.

Marketing can also include educating your customers in how you (and they) are working to better the environment. More and more, businesses are taking the opportunity to print (in non-petroleum-based ink) information about how and why such activities and products are good for the environment. If people understand why they are recycling and why they may be spending a little more on a product because it is organic, or greener in some manner, they are much more likely to want to be involved.

All in all, green marketing is ripe with opportunities to spread the word about what you do and how and why your products or services can benefit the environment. It is about utilizing greener means of marketing, which may mean opting for electronic catalogs instead of the printed versions or finding other ways to minimize the amount of paper promotional materials you use. It is about a point of view, a mindset, an attitude, and a consciousness that is permeating our culture. Consumers are entering a greater awareness than ever before and as a business owner, you want to tap into that awareness for the sake of your business and the planet.

# Having a Plan

Your marketing plans, including your promotion and advertising, will evolve through several phases, some of which may overlap. These phases are predicated by the various objectives. For example, in the beginning you will want to introduce your business, define your brand, and promote (and advertise) your products or services. Along with all of this, you will want to market the fact that you are passionate about the environment. Some businesses try to establish who they are even before introducing specific products, while other companies look to establish name recognition while presenting a line of products or selection of services. The way in which you present your business, your brand, your products, and/or services as well as your environmental commitment should be spelled out in a marketing plan, which can be officially written up or unofficial, but clearly communicated to those in a position to make such marketing and promotional efforts a reality.

You will want to think ahead, beyond your initial foray into the business world. "I'm always working on new products," says Nell Newman of Newman's Own Organics. "It's a grow-or-die industry so you should always have something up your sleeve. For us, the most recent were the peanut-butter-filled Newmanos, the tea, and our pet foods," she says.

# Promoting Products and Services

What type of promotional items will interest your target market? If, for example, you want to market your products to the 18 to 25 demographic group, you will look at the promotional items and messages that they want to hear. If, however, you are trying to market your services to an over-40 crowd, you will use different promotional and advertising messages.

Let's start by considering some promotional options. One popular means of getting your business out there is by putting your company name on promotional items, such as T-shirts, cloth or canvas bags, cups, or a host of other items, most of which can be purchased from relatively inexpensive bulk distributors and made of green materials. Products such as cloth bags and cups can be advantageous as they replace environmentally unfriendly paper and plastic bags or Styrofoam cups. Giveaway items are a means of advertising as your customers wear or carry around your company name.

Other than tangible goods, you can also give away free downloads and other electronic freebies to be cost effective. Discounts and coupons also can be a means of catching the attention of potential customers; you can use recyclable paper and soy ink for printing coupons.

Another marvelous way of promoting your business is by using your expertise in a given field, as well as ways in which people can benefit the environment. Such low-cost promotional ideas include:

- volunteering to speak at seminars or conferences.
- holding your own seminars or lectures.
- writing articles for local publications, newsletters, and/or websites in your industry.
- starting a blog about your business and perhaps your green ideas.
- writing a book about your business, your industry, and/or how you have gone green. Gary Erickson, the founder and owner of Clif Bar, wrote a book called *Raising the Bar, Integrity and Passion in Life and Business*—the story of Clif Bar & Company.
- promoting your business in discussion groups and chat rooms.
- doing interviews for the local media, including radio, television, websites, newspapers, and magazines.

"We travel all over the world doing health lectures and seminars, promoting healthy skin care and our products," explains Shelly Hiestan, who, along with her husband Denie, founded Electric Body Skin Elixar. The result is that they are getting numerous distribution deals in spas and health clinics and building a global presence.

The key to effective promotion is to do something, say something, or give away something that generates attention, while not costing you much money. The Hiestans, for example, are firm believers in healthy skin care products, and Denie, a health consultant, has worked long and hard in the field to develop the products that they sell. Likewise, Nell Newman learned about growing natural foods as a youngster and has great passion for the subject having learned all about what goes into the foods we eat. Opening an organic food business was, therefore, based on her own strong commitment to organic foods. You'll find that it is much easier to promote your green business if your marketing message comes from the heart.

As for how to promote your green business practices; most business owners will agree that it is advantageous to focus on what you have done, rather than make promises about what

## Smart Tip

You can look for trade shows by industry, state, or country at biz tradeshows.com, which even lists green shows. You can also look at local calendars and event listings for your industry by doing a search for trade shows in your area. If you find listings of last year's show, find out who presented it and contact them for information about the next show. With due diligence you should be able to find shows far enough in advance that can benefit your business. You can also go to tradeshows.com, which is a portal for trade show information.

you will do in the future. Businesses have learned the hard way, with a host of negative publicity, not to make promises that they may not be able to keep. "The best thing people can do is be true to their values, don't greenwash, but also don't be afraid to be too green because everyone and their brother is saying they are green now, and you'll want to differentiate yourselves," says Chris Bartle of The Evergreen Group LLC, involved in the buying and selling of green businesses.

Trade shows are a great way to promote your goods, as well as to network and make concrete deals. Almost every industry has trade shows, and in some cases, general shows such as AmericasMart or area home shows, which attract a variety of business owners. Paying for, designing, and setting up a booth can be costly, but very effective at the right shows, so do your research. Likewise, look for environmental fairs and similar gatherings where you can be seen sporting your green goods and/or services. Prepare the necessary literature and other materials, including green business cards (made from recyclable materials), and be well prepared prior to attending such shows.

Demonstrations of products and services are a marvelous means of promoting what you make, sell, and do. Numerous health food stores introduce new items with in-store demonstrations, while massage chairs in offices, malls, and at other locations draw customers for brief back and neck massages, promoting spas and legitimate massage businesses. The point is, seeing is believing. Toy manufacturers love to have their products spinning, flying, or bounding around in toy stores where kids can see the hot new items in action. Supermarkets have in-store food samples from their distributors. At malls or other popular locations, in-person demonstrations can be effective.

There is also the concept of free samples, especially when it comes to natural or organic foods. Inu Treats, makers of all natural goodies for pets, started out at the street fairs in Seattle, giving away treats. This allowed them to do some test marketing and make some modifications based on the overall canine response. Within a couple months of giving out free samples, store owners were asking about carrying the treats.

In the course of setting up your promotions, you'll want to pay close attention to several key factors, including:

- *Your costs*. Make sure you can afford to give away discounts, coupons, freebies, or promotional items. Stay within a realistic budget.
- *Time of year*. While your business may not be "seasonal," most businesses do have peaks and valleys. Plan promotions accordingly. You'll want to draw customers at peak times of year, and/or do special promotions to increase business during the slower times. This will depend on your business. For example, no matter how good the promotion, a ski school will be unlikely to draw many customers between June and August.
- *Your schedule*. Regardless of the time of year, you'll want to have definitive beginnings and endings to most of your promotional campaigns. This will help you measure your effectiveness and plan accordingly.
- *Your competition*. Be aware of what your competitors are doing to promote their products and services and keep pace.
- *News and events*. Businesses have their own news and events, which can range from introducing a new product to upgrading from 15 percent wind power to 65 percent wind power. Promotions can also be in line with what is newsworthy in your business, as well as within your industry. For example, in the automobile industry, if you are selling cars and a brand new hybrid makes its debut, you may want to plan a promotion in conjunction with the manufacturer and the debut of the new car.

# Public Relations

There are publicists and there are green publicists, working with more electronic press releases and less paper. Greener PR firms are becoming easier to find, operating in an environmentally friendly manner and sharing your goals for sustainability. Not only are they trying to save their own energy expenditure, but working to promote your green endeavors.

Of course not all new entrepreneurs can afford the prices of major PR firms, green or otherwise. Many PR firms ask for large monthly retainers, and many do not generate enough results to make such fees worthwhile. Therefore, you need to look for a publicist or PR firm that can work with you, understanding that you are a new business and that your funds are limited. Several PR firms, including Orca Communications and Sally Sheppard PR, were helpful in finding new up and coming green businesses to feature in the 22 green businesses highlighted in this book.

There are also many things small business owners can do to promote themselves and generate publicity on their own. Few business owners actually take the time to reach out and generate publicity even by simply sending out press releases. Many business owners will say the same things:

I don't know how to write a press release.

Nobody's going to be interested in what we're doing here.

---

## Define Your PR Objectives

**B**efore you start writing press releases, you'll want to define your PR objectives. These are your reasons for generating newsworthy stories and what you are seeking. In some cases you are seeking to establish a brand, while in others it is about a good company reputation, or simply about sales. Your public relations objectives can include:

- building awareness of what your business is all about.
- establishing your brand.
- promoting an event or activity that highlights your business.
- emphasizing your green eco-friendly objectives.
- defining what makes your business special.
- presenting a unique business story (which could be how you came to start this business in the first place).
- presenting new products and/or services.

Your message will vary depending on your public relations objective. However, it's important that there be one main message that you want to get across since mixed messages or multiple messages can be confusing.

---

I don't know who I would send a press release to.

I don't have the time to do press releases.

What business owners often do not realize is the impact of good press. A few well-placed magazine, web, or television stories can generate hundreds, if not thousands, of inquiries. The reality is that more than half of the stories you see and hear in the media are the result of good public relations.

Today, green press releases are far more prevalent. They are sent to publishers, editors, producers, and others electronically. Of course they still need to have the impact of a traditional "in-print" press release. The concept behind a press release is providing the media with a story focused on something newsworthy about your business. The reasoning behind a press release is to gain free publicity in the media, rather than simply paying for advertising. While people do buy millions, if not billions, of dollars worth of products from advertisements, the same is true from media stories, including articles in print and coverage on television, radio shows, and on the internet. The two big differences are:

1. You save a lot more money if you can generate press on your own (rather than just spending money on ads, which, very likely, you will also be doing).

2. The news comes from someone else. A journalist, reporter, news writer, or content provider writing about your business presents a more subjective third party approach than advertisements.

# Press Releases 101

Press releases are not all that difficult to write and can generate immediate attention for a new business. The goal is to promote your own company news within the short (typically one to one and half page) press release. With a little practice you, too, can write a good press release, and if you visit many business websites (especially those of larger, established companies) you'll find press sections, which often have some of the company's press releases available to read. You can also check out websites like PR Web for numerous samples of press releases indexed by industry. Another option is to look at your word processing program. Many software programs, such as Microsoft Office, include press release templates. If you'd prefer, you can look at a couple of samples that we've included at the end of this chapter. Use existing press releases that you find as templates to follow as you write your own. Note the ones that draw your attention. You'll immediately see that some get to the point immediately, while others do not "grab" you. Some are written in a reader-friendly manner with easy-to-understand terminology and not industry jargon.

The key to writing a good press release, especially one that will be sent electronically, is to generate attention with a good title and a good opening paragraph that succinctly includes the most important aspects of your story. Keep in mind that editors, producers, and freelance writers get numerous press releases.

Personally, I receive at least three or four everyday and on some days about a dozen will show up in my inbox. I hit delete on those releases for topics that I do not write about. Essentially this means that the people sending them did not do sufficient research. You should look for editors, writers, and producers who handle the industry that you are in. You need to have a targeted media list, meaning a list of contacts that meets your business needs, such as golf magazines and website editors if you are selling golf apparel. I also delete those press releases that do not give me a clear indication from the title or the first few sentences of what they are about. Remember, time is limited for those receiving many press releases at once.

Formatting a press release is simple. Use a familiar standard 12-point font such as Times New Roman or Arial and double space. Avoid anything fancy including colors. On the upper left side, print: FOR IMMEDIATE RELEASE. Also include all contact information on each page of your press release. If you print the release, use company letterhead so you will have your full contact information there.

Then it's time for your headline, which will be in larger type, and printed directly across the top of the press release. It is one of the more important aspects of the press release because you want to grab the attention of the reader. The headline could be in the form of a question, a statement that reveals part of the news, a quote, or a statistical fact. Use something that you think will make readers stop and want to read more. Don't try to be too cute, too offbeat, or too cryptic in your message. Yes, you can be clever, but in a manner that does not take away from the message.

Under the headline, you can use a sub-headline that reveals a little more information about your main marketing message or answers the question your headline has posed. The subhead should be used to provide more information that generates additional interest from the readers. Of course you don't have to have a subhead at all.

The first paragraph needs to grab the reader by making your message sound exciting without using a lot of "hype." No, your product is not the greatest thing ever. It does, however, have some important qualities that make it unique, such as being the first organic toothpaste or a new hybrid car that gets incredible gas mileage. This is where you highlight what it is that you want everyone to read about. What will make readers stop and read? What will make the TV viewers pay attention? What will have the web surfer bookmark? In two or three sentences you want to make your message clear and to the point, and you want to write in an uplifting manner. Again, avoid hype.

The next paragraphs are where you explain the who, what, where, when, and why, like a newspaper reporter. When and why was this product or service developed, how does it provide a solution to some problem that your customers might be having, and so forth. A new environmental cleaning service, for example, was developed because too many employees complain of fatigue and headaches from the poor air quality in their offices. By cleaning with only nontoxic, natural, and organic products, you leave an office environment with health-friendly air quality that benefits everyone. This paragraph should run about four or five sentences and tell the rest of the story. It should make the reader want to do a story on you based on new and interesting information. You can use a couple more paragraphs to continue explaining the highlights of the story, which might include the background of the product or service and/or the creators.

The last paragraph is what is called a boilerplate, meaning you can use this one over and over again. This should be about three or four sentences about your business. This is where you can mention how long you've been around, what you are doing that is green, and anything else significant about your company.

One of the toughest things about writing press releases is "writing short" or editing down paragraphs so that they don't run on and on. Remember, editors, writers, producers at news programs, and content managers of websites have limited time to read each and every press release that comes in and, like me, will delete plenty of them.

Conclude the press release with a call to action and contact information. A call to action means something that suggests that the reader may want to write about (or do a story on) your service, product, or newsworthy information and that you (or someone from your company) will be available for interviews.

Of course a press release is meaningless if you do not have places to which you can send it. Therefore, you will need to research local publications, appropriate websites, talk radio stations and local, or even national, television programs. Some due diligence will find you the names of the right editors, TV or radio show producers, or web content managers. It's important to first zero in on newspaper, magazine, TV and radio stations, as well as websites that are popular with your target audience. For example, finding a magazine or website that is popular among your target market is great, but if you are selling food or a dining experience, you then need to call or e-mail and ask for the name and e-mail address for the food editor. Zero in on the best people to reach with your electronic (or print) press releases. If more people did this, I wouldn't get press releases for topics that I don't write about.

Press releases could be written about many things, such as:

- launching new or improved products and services
- community involvement, such as events, sponsorships, and/or charity drives
- special recognition, such as winning an environmental award
- health and safety news and information

- contests, promotions, and special events
- results of polls, surveys, or other information that you have researched that is new and of interest to the public.
- business milestones, such as five years in business or the 1,000th customer served
- success stories regarding customers, such as thanks to their efforts a major corporation was able to go from traditional to wind power and save millions of dollars.
- celebrity involvement (which can include local personalities) who have either benefited from your products or services, or become your spokesperson.
- a unique, perhaps green discovery or invention.

## A Few Final PR tips

1. If you write your own press releases, make sure to edit and proofread carefully before sending. Remember, spellcheck doesn't catch everything.
2. Make sure your contact information is on each page.
3. If you are hiring a PR company, make sure you find out exactly where your money is going and have them provide reports on what they are doing and how much time it is taking them to do the work. You can also opt for a freelance press release writer—look at his or her work before you hire anyone. A single press release should cost between $50 and $150.
4. Save testimonials from satisfied customers, they can be included in press releases, on packaging, and so on.
5. If you have photos, several press releases, and have generated some print or online stories, you can put together a media kit. This is essentially a collection of all of the above in a nice folder designed with your company name and logo on it. These are costlier to send, but worthwhile for important clients or key potential clients. Use recycled paper. You may also include a "backgrounder," which is a one-page history of the company.

Whether it is through press releases, press kits, word of mouth, or a combination of all of these means, generating press can enhance your business in a far more cost effective manner than advertising. In fact, often one article or mention in the news leads to another. Many companies have become widely known from articles and mentions in magazines. Pangea Organics has been featured in *Entrepreneur, Food & Wine, VegNews, Time Out New York, Time, Elle, Country Home, Town & Country, Newsweek, O, Self, Jane Spa, Natural Health, Vogue, Good Housekeeping,* and other publications.

**Beware!**

When writing press releases and spreading the word about your business in newsletters or elsewhere, don't fall into the trap of self-indulgence. Too often, business owners can get caught up in the internal happenings of the company and think that such internal information is important to everyone else. Think about what other people will want to read. The fact that you just purchased a new computer system is not important to anyone outside of your home office. The fact that you planted and created the dazzling lawn sculptures on the front lawn of the mayor's house that won a prestigious award is newsworthy.

Send them to as many good (targeted) contacts as possible and don't worry about sending various releases to the same place periodically (every few weeks or each month is fine). Often persistence pays off and in some cases just letting an editor, writer, or producer know what you are up to on an ongoing basis can land you a feature article, because they see the cumulative effects of your environmental efforts and activities.

At the end of a press release, you'll usually find the word "end" or ###, a symbol signaling the end.

# Your Company Website

It's very rare that you will find a business today without a web presence. Whether it is through one page, or an elaborate website, your business needs to be represented on the web. "We've picked up 40 meetings with potential jobs in the past couple of weeks since the site launched," noted Aaron P. Levinthal, co-owner of GreeNow, who put the "green" into green events. Many business owners will echo Levinthal regarding the power of the web to draw business.

A website for a green business should be green unto itself, meaning a minimal number of energy-wasting activities, such as Flash and detailed graphics, which slow computers down. Additionally, your website is a great place to talk about your green efforts and encourage viewers and potential customers to also go "green." There are numerous ways to design a site, but as a business owner, you should opt for a professional site designer, as noted earlier, so that your website has the same high quality look as your competitors'. One of the best features of the web is that a small business can have the same web presence as a huge corporation and in many cases can have a more user-friendly, easy-to-navigate website. Since there are many places from which to learn about site design, we won't go into great detail here. Instead here are ten web tips for your new business:

1. *Leave some white space on your web pages.* Cleaner looks better than clutter.
2. *Lose the jargon.* People are growing tired of numerous companies that provide "business speak," so give them something that's straightforward.

▲

3. *If you're selling, provide product information on landing pages, meaning more details for each product* (much as Amazon.com does when you click on a book, or another product, that interests you).

4. *Highlight your green products, services, and/or accomplishments.* Don't make green promises that you do not know you can keep. Many green businesses today have sections talking about the environment and/or their products and what makes them green. Odorzout, for example, has a page on the site called "How it works," which explains how the natural mineral Zeolites helps eliminate odors.

5. *Get web visitors involved.* Have surveys, polls, trivia, or anything that keeps them coming back to participate. Jennifer Doob of Wild Dill sells all-natural and organic children's clothing and toys. With that in mind, she has a section where parents can send in pictures of their little ones. The parents will then tell everyone they know to go to the website and see a photo of their baby on the web! It's a great, fun way to draw more traffic to the site without having to pay to optimize.

6. *Use "Forward to a friend" in key areas so that they can send information about your site to their buddies and, in essence, help you do some free marketing.*

7. *Include content, such as articles or tips on how to do something.* Even brief "Top 10" lists or anecdotes can provide a reason for visitors to return to your site.

8. *Update your website often.* Stale websites do not get return visitors.

9. *Use some photos but don't overdo it.* Again, you do not want a site that loads slowly, thus using up more energy.

10. *If you link to another business, make sure you know all about that business before agreeing to link to their site.*

# Online Newsletters

A marvelous, environmentally sound means of marketing your products and services, as well as your brand identity is through an online newsletter. It's not difficult to put together a short bi-weekly or monthly newsletter to your list of subscribers. You can first build your subscription base from your website as well as your bricks-and-mortar location or through your advertising and other promotion. All you want subscribers to do is provide their e-mail address with permission for you to send your newsletter. You might, if necessary, offer a discount or some small inventive for signing up, as Wild Dill does by using the following on their website:

SAVE 15%! Sign up for the Wild Dill newsletter and receive a discount code in your e-mail box for 15% off of your next order. Get the latest Wild Dill news and save!

Online newsletters are green because they do not use paper and take minimal time to produce on your computer. The key is to lay out a newsletter in such a way that you are providing more than simply ads and promotional material. Most newsletters draw interest because of their content, which need only be a couple of short, three-paragraph stories on something pertaining to your industry. Again, you can use short tips, lists, and other means of providing content that is not necessarily in "story" form. If, for example, you are selling organic clothing, you might have a list of the top five organic materials and which ones are best for different times of year. Perhaps you are selling gourmet foods; why not write two paragraphs on some organic wines that go with your foods, or include a recipe in each newsletter? You can stockpile short articles as they come to you and/or hire someone to write your newsletter. In some cases, employees are happy to provide short tidbits to fill up a newsletter or the HR department takes on the job. However you get it done, provide just enough content to make people want to continue receiving the newsletter.

Around your content, you can put all of your upcoming promotions and below your content you can advertise as you like. Remember, it need not be very long, but a newsletter should be fresh each time and hold the reader's interest. This means writing about what's interesting to your target market. Here are a few other tips for an online newsletter:

- *Include some green activities and information.* Your business is green so you should be able to provide some green bits of information, whether it is what your business is doing for the environment or some important environmental facts.

- *Use the name of the newsletter and your business name as the subject and "from" line.* If someone in the company is in charge of the newsletter and uses his or her name, that can be unfamiliar to your readers . . . and it may be deleted.

- *Include some polls, surveys, and other interactive means of keeping your customers involved.* Asking for feedback or suggestions is a plus.

- *Avoid anything that will cause the newsletter to load slowly, such as elaborate graphics.*

- *Include a privacy paragraph assuring readers that you will not sell their e-mail address to spammers, or anyone else for that matter.*

- *Make unsubscribing easy.* No, you don't want them to unsubscribe, but if they want to, let them do so with a couple of clicks of the mouse. Many people

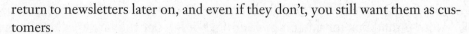
return to newsletters later on, and even if they don't, you still want them as customers.

• Consider offering a few newsletters for people with different interests.

# Blogging

Some people love blogs and others hate them. They range from well-written content on a host of interesting topics to incessant rambling. If you are passionate about the environment, a green blog is a great way to discuss your personal passion about a specific area, whether it's cleaner energy or recycling products. Stay focused, write regular blog entries and back up what you have to say with facts and data. Good blogs draw readers. The biggest problem for some is finding the time to keep on blogging. For a lowdown on starting a blog, check out Badi Jones's article at howtostart ablog.com.

Sometimes, being a part of someone else's blogs can generate a lot of attention, while saving you the time spent writing. Jennifer at Wild Dill sends samples of her organic children's products to some of the blog writers who review children's clothing and other products. This way she gets some of her products into their blogs. Look for bloggers who are writing in areas that could include your product or services. And look for green bloggers. They are always looking for new and innovative green ideas, activities and products.

# Advertising 101

Most businesses, especially new ones, need to be very careful about how they spend their advertising dollars.

Successful advertising means having an objective and reaching your target audience with the right message for the right price. Before you can create advertising copy or start determining where you will advertise, you need to consider what type of message you are trying to present. For example, will you be selling some basic and very familiar products? If so, you may want to splash your name all over the place for brand identification. Perhaps you are introducing a greener way of doing something routine or a green version of a familiar product. This will mean presenting an advertising campaign that offers the green benefits of your service or product. It is always advantageous to tout your competitive edge, which sets your service or products apart from your competitors (green or otherwise). In some cases, you are advertising a new version of a familiar product. You'll want to emphasize what makes this version faster, more powerful, and/or greener. The point is, have a plan for your advertising.

As a new business, part of your advertising objective will be to introduce yourself . . . do this in a manner that will grab the attention of the reader, listener, or viewer without detracting from the message. We've all seen ads that are very entertaining, but we immediately forget what the product was. This defeats the purpose of advertising.

For most small businesses, advertising usually means fliers, brochures, signage, print ads, websites, and perhaps some radio. Television is costly and since advertising is most effective when done on an ongoing basis, it is very hard to afford a block of television ads unless you get a great deal, which often means a very local station at a very late night hour.

## Fliers, Brochures, and More

Being green, you'll want to consider whether you want to go the flier or the brochure route. Yes, you can use nonpetroleum-based inks and recyclable paper. However, there

### Smart Tip

As when hiring a web designer (discussed earlier), if you are hiring an advertising agency or simply an experienced copywriter, know ahead of time what it is you are looking for. The more you leave up to the agency or copywriter, the more risk you take that your message will not be adequately presented. You can write your own ads or hire an expert. Either way, outline what you want to do ahead of time. Also, try to show a consistency in your ads. You will notice that most successful advertising campaigns have a theme, such as Geiko's ongoing concept of being smarter than a caveman.

is still an energy expenditure in the printing process and a time factor in distributing such one-to-one advertising. Signage on environmentally-friendly materials can also be a good way to inexpensively post your message in key locations. Posters at construction sites and even signs on benches or busses can often be affordable and very effective. Make sure that you have someone with a background in graphic design to help you with brochures and even signage. Remember, your image is reflected in everything you put out to the public. With that in mind, try to maintain a consistency in the look of your ads.

## Newspapers and Magazines

Small newspaper ads, or those in Pennysavers can be very cost effective. However, you need to make sure your ad is placed in the right category and concisely grabs the attention of your readers. Most newspapers are not very green, so take that into consideration. To locate newspapers, magazines, and specialty publications for advertising purposes, you can visit News Link at newslink.org. (You'll also find radio and TV stations there as well.)

You will find that there are more green magazines than newspapers, and that local magazines can be a good place to post an ad introducing your business to the community, perhaps with a discount or incentive of some kind. Keep in mind there is typically a long lead time for magazines, so if you want to run an ad for the end of year holiday season, you should inquire about advertising rates in June or July and ask when you need to have the copy handed in. Also keep in mind the readership of the magazine. Check the circulation numbers to make sure the ad is worth the price. Look for someone with advertising experience to layout a magazine ad, since it can be very effective if done correctly.

Also, when advertising in magazines or newspapers, get tear sheets, which are copies of the ads in print to make sure it ran correctly.

## The Internet

Online advertising can be highly effective, since people who are on the internet already are just a click away from your website. Of course, you need to find sites that target your potential buying market. "I advertise on mothering.com," says Jennifer Doob of Wild Dill. "I also look for organic parenting sites," adds Doob, who also advertises on Google's Addwords and on Yahoo, which has a similar pay-per-click offer. Search engines allow you to buy ads that work on a pay-per-click basis and come up only under appropriate searches. If done correctly—to come up only under the key words for your products and/or services—this can draw a lot of business to your website. However, if you are not set up to sell directly and easily from your site, you may be spending more money than you will make. Therefore, only do this if you are an e-tailer or a bricks-and-mortar business with a strong web-selling presence.

**Beware!**
Don't buy web ads that will result in you becoming one of those annoying pop-ups that appear on the screen when people are in the middle of reading something else. First, many programs, including anti-virus software have pop-up blockers. Secondly, like SPAM, you will alienate potential customers.

Internet ads need to grab the attention of the viewer. Make sure your message is clear and to the point since people move around the web very quickly. Also make sure to be well positioned on web pages.

## Radio

If you are a radio listener then you know there are two types of advertisements common to the medium. First are produced ads, which can be inexpensive to make but have a great impact, if they are clever and concise. Then there is written copy read by the DJ or talk show host. This can be less expensive and, if carefully written, can make your business come to life. Remember, most radio personalities are good at reading copy.

Just as with most types of advertising, the trick is to advertise often so that the public gets used to hearing your company name. Although I hate the word pithy, it does define advertising copy for radio. You want to be concise, entertaining, and promote your business in a few lines with the phone number and/or website repeated at least twice in the 15 or 30 seconds of copy.

Focus on your green edge and whatever it is that makes your business stand out. The key to a good advertisement is to emphasize or accentuate the positives. What is it that your listeners want to hear from you? Are they looking for the lowest prices? Are they looking for a green alternative to a traditional product? Are they looking for a new product or service? Are they waiting for a special deal? Do they just need to know that you exist and are open for business? Whatever you are trying to say, you can get the message across in your radio ad.

However, before buying air time, look for stations, and even specific talk shows, frequented by your target audience. A product geared for the 15-to-25-year-old market might be right for a rock station, while a product bought by a 40- to 49-year-old market might be better for a financial or news talk station or a financial talk show. If you're selling sporting goods, go for a sports station. Fit the product to the demographic audience and then see what kind of deal you can get on several spots. Typically, the more spots you buy, the cheaper the rate.

# Television

Getting on television should be left to your publicist or the work of your own PR campaign. The idea should be for you to be in the guest seat on talk shows, especially with more and more environmental programming. However, if you want to go the TV advertising route, know in advance that it can be expensive, not only to buy time, but to produce a professional-looking ad. As with radio, you want to get your message across in a short, entertaining, or engaging manner that makes it clear what it is that you are offering and why. Again, remember the high points of your product or service. Also, because people are very quick with their remotes, you can capture more potential viewers by having the name of your business, your logo, or one of your products on screen in the opening three

**Smart Tip** *Tip...*
You might check out Lorrie Morgan-Ferrero at Red Hot Copy (redhotcopy.com) for some books, software, and classes on copywriting, including copy aimed at environmentally conscious and green consumers. You also might check out Phila Hoopes at your-words-worth.com for more on green copywriting.

147

seconds of the commercial. At least this way, even if the viewer hits the remote, you've put your product (or company name) in front of them. Too many TV-ad producers make the mistake of thinking that a viewer is going to sit there through a 20-second build-up to their product. Unless the build-up is fascinating, you'll lose half of the viewers who are quick with their remote finger.

If you can buy time in blocks, even late at night, you can sometimes get a good deal. The problem you'll face is that it is difficult to get the time you want and advertising during reruns of "Mr. Ed" at 2 A.M. might not get you very many customers.

# Headlines

In most advertising, the headline is the key. This could translate to the opening five seconds on television or radio. The point is, in a short-attention-span world, you need to grab potential buyers quickly. There are plenty of books on writing advertising copy. You can purchase one and/or look closely at headlines and ad copy and watch television commercials with a new awareness of what grabs your attention and what does not. Put yourself in the place of a prospective car buyer for example, and see which of the many car advertisements on television would encourage you to shop for that model car. See which magazine or online ads catch your attention and make you read beyond the headline. Sure, the art of writing good headlines and enticing advertising copy takes some time to master, but you can get a jump on the competition by honing your skills with some practice and by knowing some of the basics.

Here are ten advertising headline and copy basics:

1. *Know what message you are trying to get across before starting.* Lower prices, higher quality, greener than your competitors, for discerning customers, etc.

2. *Know your target audience and speak their language.*

3. *Avoid stereotypes or anything that is not considered politically correct.*

4. *Don't forget to focus on the sale.* Don't be so cleaver that the reader, viewer, or listener doesn't know how or where to buy your product or service.

5. *Focus on ads that are timely, seasonal if necessary, and current.*

6. *Don't overload your headline or copy*—concise and to the point sells.

7. *Re-read copy several times to make sure it sounds, or reads, as intended.* There are many stories of advertising campaigns that were pulled from the airwaves because they were "unintentionally" suggestive or just plain offensive to someone or everyone.

8. *Be consistent.* The image or brand you create needs to remain consistent, through your design, look, tone, and message. The reason that brands must be consistent is that they take a long time to build, maintain, and evolve. This combined consistency is what builds consumer awareness of your business.

9. *Focus on a good headline.* Numbers in headlines are usually a plus, such as "10 Greener Ways to Clean Your Kitchen," and questions tend to be popular, such as "Want to Cut 30% Off Your Energy Bills?" Play with several headlines before deciding on one. You can even test market a few with friends, family, and/or your employees.

10. *Spread your advertising dollars around.* Don't rely on only one location, or even one medium to get your message out to the public.

When you plan your advertising campaign, start with a realistic budget and stay within those parameters. Otherwise, you'll find that advertising costs can add up quickly. Look for low-cost opportunities and, if buying in bulk, ask for discounts on the number of ads you are running. You can always ask for 30 percent off and settle for 10 percent. It doesn't hurt to try negotiating, especially if you are close to the deadline and their advertising space is not filled. Also, don't forget cooperative advertising can work for you. This is where you and another business advertise together. Often manufacturers and stores that sell the manufacturer's products participate in co-op advertising programs. This saves you half the money and allows you to place more ads online or in print.

In the end, advertising can work if you are able to maintain the costs and build a campaign that generates attention. For many new business owners, low-cost publicity options will still prevail over advertising, especially if you are doing something good for the environment and spread the word. Several major magazines have green issues, including *Elle*, *Vanity Fair*, and *Parents*, plus numerous websites are doing green issues or adding green sections. Articles, as well as awards, TV, radio, and online interviews, or (positive) mentions in the news are marvelous ways to boost your business, as Carolyn Deal from Sum-Bo-Shine, makers of organic baby products, can attest to. "Sum-Bo-Shine Naturals and Organics were honored as the 'Going Green Champion'" by ABC News in Atlanta, Georgia. "That was far more coverage than we could have gotten with a few ads and much less costly," says Deal.

# Sample Press Release #1

Sample Press Release, courtesy of Orca Communications Unlimited, LLC

## REVOLUTIONARY NEW PRODUCTS LEAVE CLOTHES CLEAN AND THE EARTH HAPPY

*—Compact Yet Powerful Washing Machines and Dryers are Turning Out Cleaner Clothing and a Cleaner Earth—*

Middletown Springs, VT—February 15, 2007—The Laundry Alternative, Inc., today announced the nationwide release and debut of the new Wonder Wash Pressure Compact Washing Machine, Spin Dryer, and Mini Countertop Spin Dryer. These revolutionary products are easy and safe to use and are working to save the environment by cutting down on water and electricity usage. Although these products serve the same function as a traditional washing machine and dryer, they do it in a radical new way. The Wonder Wash and Spin Dryer clean and dry clothing in compact and affordable machines.

Responding to a growing need for affordable, earth friendly products, The Laundry Alternative has created a practical answer. The innovative machines save consumers money, as much as $150–$250 per year. The Wonder Wash uses 90 percent less water and detergent than conventional washing machines and fits easily on any countertop. The Spin dryer can cut 5 to 10 percent of an annual household's energy use, making this revolutionary new product over 100 times more energy efficient than a traditional tumble dryer. The Laundry Alternative is committed to creating innovative, cost-saving, environmentally friendly products that work. According to founder Corey K. Tournet, "We continuously research and develop new energy-saving laundry products. Our newest product is a spin dryer which can dramatically cut average household energy consumption, and we have many more new laundry inventions in the pipeline."

The Laundry Alternative has created a positive reaction from consumers around the world. The Wonderwash has made an impact on the American soldiers fighting in Iraq and Afghanistan, who don't have access to washing machines or a reliable laundry service. Each product is created with care and is inspected by a company with over 10 years experience before being released to the public. Owner Corey K Tournet states, "One of our main goals is to provide practical, inexpensive laundry solutions to people who do not have access to conventional washers and dryers in their homes, such as apartment dwellers."

## Sample Press Release #1, continued

About Laundry Alternative, Inc.

The Laundry Alternative, Inc. is located in Middletown Springs, Vermont. Created by Corey K Tournet in 1999, the company is committed to providing the consumer with innovative, cost-saving, environmentally friendly products that work. The Laundry Alternative, Inc. has been recognized by numerous media publications and continues to make an impact on consumers and the environment.

For more information, please visit the corporate web site at

laundry-alternative.com

For press inquiries, please contact Kirstin Sanders, Senior Publicist, Orca Communications at (480) 363-5371 or KSanders@OrcaCommunications.com.

# # #

# Sample Press Release #2

Sample Press Release, courtesy of Orca Communications Unlimited, LLC

## ODORZOUT RECEIVES THE U.S. ENVIRONMENTAL PROTECTION AGENCY'S SEAL OF APPROVAL

*—All natural odor-removal products recognized as environmentally friendly by the Design for the Environment Program—*

Phoenix, AZ—January 28, 2008—No Stink, Inc., announced today their line of ODORZOUT odor-removal products has been selected as a partner of the U.S. Environment Protection Agency's Design for the Environment (DfE) Program. DfE officially acknowledged ODORZOUT as an environmentally safe product having adhered to their strict partner guidelines that recognize and encourage the formulation of products with environmentally preferred chemistry.

ODORZOUT was selected based on the products' blend of all-natural Zeolite minerals, which exhibits a more positive effect on the environment than conventional odor removers. ODORZOUT's complete line of odor remover products has qualified for the DfE Program, including All Surface Granules, All Purpose Pouch, Laundry Additive Powder, Foot Powder, Pet All Surface

Granules, Pet Pouch, Cat All Surface Granules, Cat Litter Additive Powder, and Cat Litter.

"We are thrilled to have ODORZOUT be a part of this important partnership," commented Barry L. Reifman, owner of No Stink, Inc. "It validates what we and our customers have always known: ODORZOUT not only works to remove odors, but it does so safely for humans, pets, and the environment. We are proud to have produced our quality line of green products from day one."

DfE commends companies such as No Stink, Inc., for their leadership in designing products that are good for their business and for the environment. The DfE Program works in partnership with a broad range of stakeholders to reduce risk to people and the environment by preventing pollution. DfE focuses on industries that combine the potential for chemical risk reduction and improvements in energy efficiency with a strong motivation to make lasting, positive changes.

About Odorzout

ODORZOUT is a line of All Natural Odor Eliminators consisting of a blend of Zeolites, nontoxic minerals that absorb and eliminate unpleasant odors. These odor removers come in powder and granule forms and contain no chemicals or perfumes and are 100 percent safe for humans and animals. ODORZOUT is ideal to use anywhere and is offered in the following forms: All Surface Granules, All Purpose Pouch, Laundry Additive Powder, Foot Powder, Pet All Surface Granules, Pet Pouch, Cat All Surface Granules, Cat Litter Additive Powder, and Cat Litter. ODORZOUT has also been endorsed by The Queen of Clean®, Linda Cobb, who has given it her official seal of approval. Additional information provided at 88stink.com.

For more information, interviews, and/or other media inquiries, please contact Marybeth Grass at Orca Communications Unlimited, LLC at 602-896-7643 or Marybeth@orcacommunications.com.

# # #

# 10

# Social
# Responsibility

Beyond the physical attributes of the earth, the green culture also extends to caring for its inhabitants. Social responsibility is defined as acting with concern and understanding for other people, particularly those who are disadvantaged. For a business, it is also the awareness of your impact on the well-being of others. This extends from doing what is best for your own employees to improving conditions for workers living halfway around the world.

# It Starts at Home

Along with health benefits, Pangea Organics does the little things, such as setting up a locker room facility where employees who bike to work can change when they arrive. As noted earlier, New Belgium Brewery gives employees bicycles after one year to encourage alternative commuting. A growing number of companies now encourage employee volunteering with pay, and many set up volunteering opportunities in conjunction with local hospitals, organizations helping underprivileged children, and so on.

By respecting your employees and incorporating a culture that emphasizes doing for others, you build a work force that cares. Surveys, such as one by Sirota Survey Intelligence, have shown that employees who are satisfied with their organization's commitment to social and environmental responsibility are more likely to have a positive attitude and be more productive than those working for employers who play a lesser role when it comes to social responsibility.

"I wanted to start a company that could be a role model for the different processes that you could put in place to become a profitable company, but do so by respecting your employees, the people making your products, the planet, and the end user as well," explains Pangea Founder & CEO, Joshua Scott Onysko, who left school at sixteen and took odd jobs for eight years, while traveling the world and learning firsthand about environmental concerns.

Along with health and medical benefits, companies are now more attuned to providing their employees with something more. Having a reputation for being socially conscious when it comes to your personnel will allow you to attract top job candidates and those that will stick around longer, showing a greater commitment to your company. Flex hours, educational programs (which can include paying part of school tuition), day care, and a greener work environment are among the most popular means of demonstrating your commitment to your employees. While wellness is not necessarily "green," health of body and mind go hand in hand with the global picture. Healthier, less "stressed" employees can benefit a business by taking fewer sick or personal days, being more mentally alert, and physically at the top of their game. From in-house medical screenings by hospital personnel to lectures and seminars on anything from diet and nutrition to high blood pressure, businesses of all sizes are taking the opportunity to make a difference for their employees. Many businesses also offer in-house yoga or aerobics classes or have fitness equipment available.

## It Pays to Care

**A**ccording to a survey by the Care2 Network (care2.com), 48 percent of employees say they would work for less pay if they could work for a socially-responsible company. In fact, 73 percent of workers responded that it is "very important" to work at a company that they believe is "socially responsible."

Companies most mentioned as "socially responsible" by survey respondents included Ben & Jerry's, The Body Shop, Patagonia, Seventh Generation, and Starbucks.

To help employees find environmentally aware and socially responsible companies, the Care2 Network has instituted the Care2 JobFinder.

The trend to move in a more socially conscious direction is not just reserved for the United States. For example, a construction company in Brazil offers its employees the opportunity to complete grade and high school education through its Basic Education Program. Over the past four years, more than 700 employees have participated and succeeded.

# Doing for Others

The number of companies aligning themselves with green and/or charitable groups is growing by leaps and bounds. Companies throughout the United States and around the world, are setting up programs and teaming with socially concerned groups and organizations allowing their employees to get involved in some manner. Clif Bar, for example, is involved with the Organic Farming Research Foundation. They also use the phrase "Make it happen" to reflect the company belief that if you care about wild places, you need to do your part to ensure they are saved for future generations. In the course of "making it happen" they have sponsored numerous programs such as their Two Mile Challenge, which was designed to promote bike riding as an alternative means of transportation. Cliff Bar & Company have also taken part in working with Habitat for Humanity and teamed with the Breast Cancer Fund on a variety of programs and events that have raised over $1.5 million dollars. All tolled, the health bar company has supported 90-plus nonprofit organizations, many focused on the betterment of the planet, while others support health- and education-related issues.

For some companies it is active participation in fund raising, or hands-on activities, while for others it is donating their products and or services. For example, Nestle Waters North America donated 222,234 half-liter bottles of Ozarka® Brand Natural Spring Water to citizens and disaster relief workers affected by Category 2 Hurricane Dolly. After Hurricane Katrina, thousands of companies pitched in and got involved in clean up, relief, and rebuilding efforts.

Again, this is not just reserved for U.S. companies but is a worldwide phenomenon. For example, in Costa Rica, a pharmaceutical company donated over one million doses of vaccines against measles, mumps, and rubella to help the Pan American Health Organization (PAHO) achieve its goal of measles eradication.

The point is, it's almost impossible today for any business, large or small, to sit on the sidelines and ignore the plight of the world. Whether it is helping alleviate the devastation of a natural disaster or helping to rebuild a rain forest, the need for social involvement is great and your business needs to get involved. Your employees, customers, and stakeholders will be glad you did.

> ## Smart Tip
>
> **Tip...**
>
> For an overview of the world of Corporate Responsibility, visit the CSRwire (Corporate Social Responsibility Newswire) at csrwire.com. CSRwire, covering issues including diversity, philanthropy, human rights, and workplace issues, is a leading source of corporate social responsibility and sustainability news, reports, and information.

# Fair Trade Practices

"It's very simple to buy fair trade coffee for your office. It costs a little more but you are helping farmers and workers in other parts of the world," says Mark A. Regier, Stewardship Investing Services Manager for Mennonite Mutual Aid (MMA). Fair trade practices refer to the support of economic justice and fairness as exemplified in the quality and pricing of products. It is designed to eliminate exploitive trade practices and assure that companies involved in the importing and exporting of goods adhere to certain predefined rules designed to make trading fair. In a free market, companies are, unfortunately, able to take advantage of international buyers. In addition, in regions of the world such as Latin America, Africa, Asia, India, and the Caribbean there are minimal rules or guidelines to protect the treatment and pay rate of the workers.

Fair trade practices are designed to protect both workers and the environment. Fair trade certification, initiated by the Fairtrade Labeling Organization International (fairtrade.net), is sourced directly from local cooperatives, which results in more money going to the growers. Part of Fair Trade Practices is to ensure that farmers, growers, and other workers are not being exploited or treated unfairly, and as a result supports a better life for these workers by guaranteeing compliance with national and regional minimum wage and labor standards.

Doing your part means looking for fair trade certified products. This indicates that workers are receiving fair wages. Starbucks, for example, pays their coffee farmers prices for beans that are above the going rate, while also working with them to use the most environmentally friendly methods of growing and harvesting the coffee beans. If in doubt about where products are coming from, do your research and find out where and how your products are being made, by whom, and at what wages. When working with crafts makers and artisans you want to make sure that they are being fairly compensated. You can also purchase goods from nonprofit groups or cooperatives of farmers, artisans, or manufacturers, which will help ensure fair pay.

In addition, seek out opportunities to support undervalued and/or underserved populations. For example, Pangea Organic supports women-owned farms, of which there are not many in the world, despite the vast number of women involved in farming and food production. Look to benefit populations that are not receiving fair pay or fair opportunities. Also research worker treatment and support only those businesses and economies that are treating workers in a humane manner.

Finally, you can give some of your profits back to indigenous populations to support and strengthen the social and economic conditions in the producer communities.

For more on Fair Trade, you can go to the Fair Trade Federation (FTF) at fair tradefederation.org or Fair Trade Certified at transfairusa.org.

# A Green Work Environment

Air quality and a healthy workplace are at the top of the list of employee concerns. Of course, if you have customers coming to your business, cleaner air and a healthy environment will spill over and affect them as well.

One of the first and foremost concerns regarding office health and clean air comes from the manner in which the office is being cleaned and the cleaning products being used. For years, traditional cleaning products have been comprised of dangerous chemicals. Such products kill germs and shine surfaces but also release toxins into the air. The cans or bottles are then discarded into landfills as hazardous waste. While these cleaning products are still on the market, a rapidly increasing number of concerned business owners and managers have opted to clean up their office environment by switching to nontoxic, less dangerous alternatives.

Along with ammonia, borax, and good old baking soda, there are green cleaning products that can do the same job as the high-powered, high-toxic cleaners. Many of these products are certified by Green Seal, an independent nonprofit organization that promotes the manufacturing, purchasing, and overall use of environmentally responsible products and services. Green Seal evaluates cleaning (and other) products and gives their seal of approval to those that meet their high standards (greenseal.org).

For your purposes, you will be seeking cleaning products that:

- have no volatile organic compounds (VOCs).
- have no ingredients derived from petroleum.
- have no chlorine bleach.
- have a neutral pH.
- have no phosphates.
- have no artificial fragrances or dyes.
- are nontoxic to humans, animals, and plants.
- are biodegradable.
- come in containers that are recyclable, refillable, or reusable.
- are made from naturally derived ingredients from replenishable sources.

Along with using greener cleaning products, the use of microfiber mops and cloths can also be beneficial to your work environment. In addition, safety procedures should be initiated and followed closely. Containers should be closed tightly, spills cleaned up immediately, and anything that needs to be disposed of should be done so in a safe manner. From the start, you need to instill good habits, including cleaning up the kitchen area and workstations so that nothing is left out that can and will contaminate a clean workspace. Don't forget that fresh air and proper ventilation are important, especially in manufacturing-based businesses.

While doing your part to prevent what is called "indoor air pollution," you will also want to consider all the potential sources of pollutant and residue that comes from:

- cleaning products
- packing materials
- technology
- foods and chemicals used on agricultural products
- dust and particles from manufacturing products.

Add to this anything brought in on the clothing of your staff, and you get the idea . . . a lot of potential pollutants fill the air in most work establishments.

There are various means of improving air quality in your workspace. Air filters can be placed strategically by return vents and in other locations. In some HVAC systems, such filters are already in place. Filters are designed to catch the particles that pass through. HEPA (High Energy Particulate Air) filters and ULPA (Ultra Low Penetration Air) filters are DEA-approved and can capture dust and other airborne particles. Should you be in the manufacturing business, you may need air-filtering systems that meet government clean air regulations.

Some basic means of maintaining cleaner air in your office includes making sure vents are not blocked, HVAC systems are cleaned out periodically, smoking is permitted in outdoor areas only, spills are cleaned up quickly, trash is kept in specified areas and covered, and cleaning products are environmentally friendly. Disposing of waste in a proper, efficient manner and making sure that any leaks or cracks in walls are repaired quickly will also help you maintain a healthy work environment.

> ⚠️ **Beware!**
> There are a lot of air purifiers on the market. Be careful, however, because those using ozone to clean the air (including UV air purifiers) may be doing as much harm as good. Ozone released into the atmosphere can defeat the purpose of trying to "purify" the air. Ionizing also releases particles into the air. Therefore, the air purifiers that you are looking for, which are the only EPA-approved filters, are the HEPA ones. Before buying any indoor air purifier, do your homework and make sure it is EPA approved.

# Green Education

Many green business owners today make a point of letting customers, stakeholders, and the community know about that which they learned about the environment. On the Wild Dill website (wilddill.com) a section called "why organic, fair, natural?" explains the importance of bamboo and soy fiber, organic cotton, and fair trade. An "environment" section on the iTySE website (ityse.biz) provides some facts and figures on the negative environmental impacts of plastic bags. The GreeNow website, (greenow.org) has a section on "Why Biodiesel?" explaining why the use of biodiesel is good for the planet, good for business, and good for your bottom line. The point is, your website is an ideal place to explain the benefits of your products and services while promoting them. Explaining how being green in your little niche of the world is your way of educating web visitors, including regular and potential customers.

You can also spread the word about local or even natural projects and initiatives taking place in the near future. Becoming a source of green information for the community puts you in a highly visible position, allowing you to benefit from promotion while letting people know how and where they can get involved in environmental activities and actions.

Taking the concept one step further, you can also sponsor local events with green themes. New Belgium Brewery has sponsored bike events, while other businesses have raised money through a variety of green activities. Hands-on local clean ups can also be a way of acting on behalf of your global concerns.

One of the most significant ways in which to make a difference is through education, and that is part of social responsibility. Share what you have learned. This may also include sharing ways in which you have learned through your own errors or by changing your ways. Even a well-intentioned green business will likely discover ways in which they can become greener and can teach others based on their own examples of greening their businesses. "Recently, we had to redo all our labels to become greener," says Barry Reifman, (aka Dr. Stink) of Odorzout, adding that this is how you keep up with the times, by learning what else you can do to be a greener company.

A very enjoyable way of spreading the "green" word is to educate students at local schools. While being an excellent way to acquaint yourself with the community, it is also very gratifying to teach children how to help save their planet. Of course you'll need to stick to a few basic topics and, depending on the age of the audience, speak their language. However, you will walk away with a rewarding feeling, especially after fielding questions about what the students can do to become junior environmentalists.

> **Tip...**
>
> **Smart Tip**
> Show people what you are up to either through tours of your facility or through talks, lectures, blogs, or a green newsletter. This allows you to teach environmentalism by painting a green picture of your company and educating not just consumers but other business owners.

# Giving Your People What They Want

In the early days of your business, you may not have many, if any, employees. You will, hopefully, have your fair share of customers as your business grows. If you want to know what your employees and/or customers want, you need to ask them. Hotels and restaurants have cards for diners and visitors to write down what they would like to see more of, or less of. You, too, can have surveys on your website, a place for suggestions, or even some printed suggestion cards. The idea is to gather input and determine which ideas might actually fly and which may not be within the scope of your business and/or your budget.

Having occasional brainstorming meetings with your staffers—even if there are only two or three of you—can be very helpful for any business, especially in the early stages. Green topics can be part of the discussion, focusing on what other ways and means of greening your business are actually feasible. You'll find that some ideas may be perfectly suited to your business as it stands now, while others may be worth hanging onto for future reference.

One note of caution: Whether it is implementing new ideas within your company or aligning yourself with environmental groups and causes, you need to be genuine. In a very web-savvy world, you can't fool most of the people most of the time. Therefore, if you say that you are going to commit to a new idea, internally or externally, follow through on it. Your employees and your customers can smell a "phoney" commitment to social responsibility a mile away, so unless you're really committed to a cause, don't try to exploit the concerns and interests of your employees or your customers to enhance your image or make a profit. The result of such foolery will very likely be a huge step back for your business.

# Socially Responsible Investing

Environmentally speaking, why not put your money where your mouth is? Socially Responsible Investing (SRI) is a means of making investment choices for your business, your employees, and yourself that reflect the values that are meaningful to the investor. Social consciousness is part of the investment criteria in Socially Responsible Investing, which has become a growing segment of the investment universe, with over $2.3 trillion in investment capital in over 200 SRI mutual funds. And this does not include other funds that are adding socially responsible companies as a means of greening their portfolios. It also does not include making investments directly in new businesses that, like yours, are environmentally aware. "Mission-driven companies can look at how they are infusing that mission through all aspects of our work, including the investments they make," says Mark A. Regier Stewardship Investing Services Manager for MMA. Businesses, as well as the individuals who own and run them, need to consider where they will invest their money, and socially responsible investment opportunities provide peace of mind.

Criteria vary when it comes to SRI funds, but most are concerned with the products, practices, and management of the businesses in which the funds are investing. Among the social issues incorporated into the stock selection criteria of most SRI mutual funds are:

- human rights
- workplace safety
- community relations and responsibility
- global responsibility, or not
- workplace discrimination

The environmental criteria include:

- type of products manufactured and/or sold
- $CO_2$ emissions or carbon footprint
- Overall sustainability of the business and concern for the environment.
- Manner of doing business, such as shipping, packaging, etc.

These criteria will vary depending on the various holdings of a mutual fund and the nature of the fund. The point is, however, that SRI funds will screen out businesses that are destroying rain forests, polluting waterways, exploiting workers, and making products that are high in toxicity. You can do the same while screening any type of investments, including stocks or investments in other local businesses.

Whether you are looking to invest personally, invest some of your company's profits down the road, or provide 401k choices for your employees, you will need to exercise some due diligence. Along with environmental concerns, you'll want to focus on the financial risks associated with all investments and look at the direction in which the market has been headed and try to determine whether you foresee a bull or bear market in the near future.

Critics of SRI, including some financial planners, will argue that perhaps you should simply invest wherever you find the greatest possible profits, make some money, and then use that money to support environmental causes. However, many

---

## Investing Language and What to Look At

**W**hen reviewing mutual funds, keep in mind that the commonly posted Average Annual Return is not as true an indicator of success as the Compounded Annual Return. The reason is that if your investment gives you a return of 14 percent over five years, you will have doubled your investment because the investment is compounding annually. Therefore, rather than 14 percent x 5 years or a 70 percent return, you would actually make a 100 percent return on your initial investment. Average Annual Returns will show you 100 percent divided by 5, or a 20 percent Average Annual Return, which isn't really the case, but looks better for those who are selling investment products. In short, you aren't really seeing a 20 percent return annually, but a 14 percent return annually and you are making more money each year because of the interest. Look for Compounded Annual Return as a better measure of accurate returns.

investors feel that you should not support companies and businesses that you do not believe are environmentally friendly or socially responsible, but instead align yourself with companies that share your beliefs and environmental vision. It's important to back businesses and companies you believe in. "Part of our investment strategy is to include investments that in and of themselves are very positive in terms of benefits to society as a whole," says Regier, adding that they do that through investing in things like responsible real estate, in which issues of the environment and benefits of certain types of construction are being considered.

When looking at SRI mutual funds, look at the holdings of the funds to see which ones include companies that are doing something you believe in. Give your employees some choices for their 401k plans and also consider ETFs. These are Exchange Traded Funds of stocks, bonds, or in some cases other types of investments, that trade on a stock exchange in much the same manner as a typical stock. Unlike mutual funds, you can trade them at any time during the day for a given price. Typically, they track an index, which means less trading, resulting in lower fees for you as the investor. ETFs are new and growing at a very rapid pace with trillions of dollars already invested. A couple of SRI examples would be:

- The *Barclays iShares KLD Select Social Index* (NYSE: KLD), which invests in companies in the KLD Select Social index. The KLD uses a set of socially responsible criteria and is comprised of 200 to 300 companies from the S&P 500 and Russell 1000 indices.
- The *Power-Shares WilderHill Clean Energy Portfolio* (AMEX: PBW), which, in its own words, "seeks to replicate, before fees and expenses, the WilderHill Clean Energy Index," which includes various companies that focus on greener and generally renewable sources of energy and technologies.

You will many find others, even some that track the PAX index (such as the Pax World Balanced Fund, considered the forerunner of the SRI fund movement), which was the first socially responsible index, formed back in 1970. And there are other SRI Indices to note, such as the Domini 400 Social Index, the Calvert Social Index, and the KLD Broad Market Social Index.

Another option is to simply invest in the stocks, or bonds issued, of companies that you believe are doing something positive for the environment. Showing support for such companies is part of socially responsible investing. In fact, SRI has lit a fire under corporate leaders to get their companies into a better position when it comes to environmental concerns. Many closed-door executive meetings are now the result of not meeting socially responsible criteria and therefore not generating the same investment dollars as in the past. This is the result of a more socially conscious investing public.

Of course SRI is subjective. For example, on one hand you might want to invest in a hotel chain that utilizes green building practices and donates to One Percent for The Planet. On the other hand, you may also consider it a negative that they serve alcohol at their hotel bars and in their in-room hospitality bars. Everyone needs to draw their own lines in the sand regarding what they believe in, and some people will include their own views on what are considered "vices," while others will stick with that which has a direct correlation to their environmental concerns—to each their own.

There is a reality factor in Socially Responsible Investing and that is that you can make cases for the degree of social responsibility for any business and any individual. To what degree is a business socially responsible or not? That is the line you draw when you set up your own criteria.

The other factors in terms of selecting socially responsible investments are the financial ones that come into play in any type of investing. You need to look at the earnings of the company or fund, the fees, the future projections, and so on. Here are six quick general investment tips:

1. *Don't invest what you don't have.* Until your business has working capital and steady cash flow, you probably won't be doing much investing. In other words, do not invest money needed for business operations or your own personal needs.

2. *Pay attention.* Too many investors simply put their money into a fund or stock(s) and "let it ride" so to speak. Follow your investments and don't be afraid to make changes if and when necessary. Holding a losing stock or fund forever (simply because you believe that "someday it will rebound"), is neither profitable or sensible.

3. *Don't follow the pack mentality.* Investing is a personal thing so you'll want to go with investments that you believe in. Remember, last year's big winners may very likely be among this year's losers (which is often the case).

4. *You do not have to be 100 percent invested at all times.* In a bear market, you might simply want to pull some of your money out, rather than watching it disappear, and put it into cash holdings until the market turns around.

5. *Take advice with a grain of salt.* Far too many people think they have the answer when it comes to making money through investments. Unless you meet someone who can truly read the future (and we know of nobody at this point, except perhaps Nostradamus) don't buy into other people's advice unless you do your research.

6. *Know your level of risk.* If a high-risk investment option will keep you up all night, give you anxiety attacks, and put you in the hospital, it isn't worth it, since the money will only go to footing your hospital bills. There's nothing

wrong with being a conservative investor if it provides you peace of mind. You may not make as much as a more aggressive investor, but you also won't lose as much. Hint: Consider stop loss orders so that your investment can only drop a small percentage (such as 5 percent) before you get out.

There are books on Socially Responsible Investing, and plenty of information available online. One place you can look at Social Funds is at socialfunds.com; another is the Social Investing Forum at socialinvest.org.

# Keeping It
## Going

**S**tarting off as a green business is admirable. It shows that you are following your passion beyond the desire to make money. The question, however, is can you sustain sustainability?

# Maintaining Positive Green Habits

By starting off on the right foot, you are able to instill good habits, in yourself, in your employees, and in your customers. In many cases, your business was built on principles that set you apart from the more traditional entrepreneur, principles that are at the core of who you are, giving you a head start and making it easier to maintain your focus.

Thinking back periodically on your initial impetus for starting a green business is a great way to maintain your environmental entrepreneurial spirit. Jennifer Doob remembers her reasoning for starting Wild Dill. "I took a year off to stay at home with my son, and I recall that when I went shopping I kept thinking that there just aren't enough organic products for babies and toddlers," explains Jennifer.

"In response to people asking for greener events, I called around and asked if anyone used biodiesel in the generators they used. Nobody did, so I started working on the idea. It [greener events] was something that people wanted but nobody was offering," says Aaron Levinthal of GreeNow.

Shawana Pierson and Chris Kodama of iTySE only need to see the sheer number of plastic bags being dispensed at various stores and discarded along the roadside or on the beach to recall their initial desire to make a difference. "This business was a response to what we have seen with the volume of plastic bags still being used. We felt that people would respond to a stylish alternative product, and so far they have," explains Shawana Pierson.

Maintaining your environmental focus is largely a matter of reflecting on the principles that got you started, which, when followed diligently and combined with a strong entrepreneurial spirit, can be the stepping stones for great success. When Jeff Lebesch and his wife Kim Jordan hiked up into the mountains to contemplate how to take their home-brewing process and turn it into New Belgium Brewery, little did they know that their 100 percent wind-powered business would also generate a tremendous amount of attention as a leader in sustainability, not to mention a very successful brewery.

# Putting It All Together (and Being Recognized)

Quality products, first-rate service, attention to your customers, watching your expenses, putting profits back into your company in the early years, having steady cash flow, and hiring good people are all significant aspects to running a successful business. You need to focus your attention on all of these areas and promote your business accordingly within your budget and to your target market. Most of the 22 green businesses profiled in Chapter 2 and discussed throughout this book are still in their growing stages. By growing slowly and steadily, they can flourish. However, each business owner needs to keep in mind the pace at which the business can realistically grow.

For some businesses, the goals are simply to stay small and earn money for the two or three people involved. For other businesses, the basement or garage is just the starting location for what will hopefully become a large company, perhaps even going public one day. It does happen. The point is to focus on both short- and long-term goals, realizing that it takes the short-term successes to reach the long-term goals. This holds true for both financial and environmental goals.

> **Tip...**
>
> **Smart Tip**
> Utilize testimonials. In your newsletter, on your advertising, and certainly on your website, testimonials can illustrate how pleased your customers were with your products or services. Odorzout, for example, has a "Testimonials" section on their website (odorzout.com). Be forewarned that all testimonials must be legitimate or you can find yourself in big trouble.

Companies like Seventh Generation, Pangea Organics, or Clif Bar have already seen significant financial returns while generating plenty of accolades for their sustainability, green activities, and social consciousness. They have been widely recognized for their efforts and, in fact, won awards. For example, in August 2008 Seventh Generation, the nation's leading seller of nontoxic household products, was named one of America's top ten favorite "green" brands by San Francisco-based marketing expert Outlaw Consulting. Of course it's not really about winning awards but making a difference. Nonetheless, awards help draw attention, which in turn helps you reach more people and make a greater difference . . . so, in a manner of speaking, it's a cyclical process.

Much smaller companies, such as Sum-Bo-Shine and WeWe Clothing will grow slowly as they generate attention for their competitive edge—having unique green products. They, too, can benefit from being recognized for their environmental contributions, WeWe Clothing was chosen by ThisNext.com as "designer of the week" and Sum-Bo-Shine was awarded Best Organic and Eco-Friendly Products for 2008 by Orca Communications Unlimited, LLC. Every little helps and recognition is a big boost for any small business.

# Staying on Top of Your Industry News

Reports of new environmentally favorable fabrics can be quite significant in the clothing industry. The latest in hybrid cars can draw great interest from car buyers. Tastier organic edibles can be a boon for the organic food seller. The point is that as an entrepreneur, you need to find your sources of industry information from day one and keep reading and learning about industry activities (green or otherwise) as you proceed in business. The successful entrepreneur knows what is coming around the bend in his or her industry and is ready to embrace new trends, or not, depending on the nature of the changes.

Almost every industry has places from which you can gather information, including:

- associations and member groups
- trade shows
- websites and discussion boards
- newsletters
- conferences
- trade magazines
- networking groups

Likewise, there are newsworthy environmental sites keeping you abreast of the latest in green activities in general and/or in your specific industry (see the reference section at the end of this book for some green websites you may want to visit).

By staying on top of the latest activities in your industry, as well as green activities, you can better position your company competitively in the market. Additionally, you do not get stale or fall behind in the ever-advancing business community. Embracing new business ideas as well as green alternatives to traditional thinking also generates greater enthusiasm for your employees and customers, who see progress and forward thinking.

# Setting Up Your Benchmarks

As your business gets off the ground, it is important to set markers, or benchmarks, if you prefer, at which times you can take a look at where you are in conjunction with your goals, as a business owner and as a responsible citizen.

Periodically, you will want to do a company check to make sure you are:

- maintaining an inventory that meets your customer's needs.
- up to date on the latest services offered.
- maintaining enough cash to purchase what you need.
- building strong relationships with your customers.
- providing incentives and positive feedback to your employees.
- managing internal problems effectively, whether they are with employees, vendors or suppliers.

- keeping track of what your competitors are up to.
- keeping a close eye on your bookkeeping.
- keeping a close eye on your tax payments.
- using cost-effective means of promotion and advertising (and staying within your budget).
- being transparent with your shareholders and incorporating their ideas and concerns into your business plans and strategies.
- dealing with suppliers.
- dealing with green suppliers as much as possible.
- doing as much as you can to conserve energy, water, and natural resources.
- considering alternative, greener means of operating your business, and/or production.
- managing waste efficiently.
- using a green purchasing policy within your facility.
- focusing on indoor air quality.
- limiting shipping and travel needs.
- promoting alternative means of commuting.
- being as sustainable as possible.
- involved in your community, through sponsorship, green activities, participation in community events, etc.

Set these up as guidelines to look at when you check to see where you are as your company grows. Try to make honest assessments and make the areas in which you are falling short top priorities for the near future.

Keeping a business afloat, especially in its early stages, while establishing your best practices, means playing the role of a juggler. As Jan McCabe, co-owner of Montana Stones, says, "Right now, we're just trying to keep all the balls in the air," referring to the business she and her husband run selling items made from natural Montana stones, while she is still maintaining another small business setting up flexible benefits plans. The hope for the McCabes, like many new business owners, is that their business grows in the wake of raised awareness of natural products.

# The Future of Green

Environmental concerns are actually not new. In the 1960s and '70s there were movements against pollution and very real concerns, but the Vietnam War, race relations, and various other issues swept the environmentalists out of the limelight. For years environmentalism was seen as counter-culture, as something that emerged from the hippie era and wasn't practical in a rapidly advancing, highly technical society. In time, however, global warming became a very real, scientifically proven concern and was documented by high-profile individuals such as Al Gore, among others. The resulting changes in weather patterns coupled with media articles about water pollution, toxins in the air, rainforests disappearing, and the truth about pesticides and the food we eat became more prevalent and began to alarm a culture that was very content ignoring that which it did not see firsthand. The internet connected the globe as never before and, within the past ten years, awareness of the environment and the concerns for the planet finally reached epic proportion.

Finally, the green masses are generating attention in circles that turned a blind eye in the past, with many companies and even politicians being forced, by the growing wave of environmental support, to take notice and subsequent action. Of course the true environmentalists can spot the greenwashers a mile away. They are those companies that are faking environmental concern or throwing their hat into the ring in order to look good. It's a dangerous game and if caught the business can lose hundreds of thousands, if not millions of dollars between boycotts and bad press.

The efforts of major corporations that are seriously trying to make a difference can certainly have a major impact, simply because they have the money, influence, and manpower to contribute. However, small businesses make up more than 80 percent of all businesses in the United States, and a large portion of the global economy as well. It is the small-business owner who can lay the foundation by shining light on the numerous environmental issues and bringing them to the attention of the large conglomerates. It is the small-business owner can make a difference in each and every community and now in the mass media thanks to the power of their presence on the internet.

Together, small-business owners can, and have, brought environmental concerns to the public as well as the politicians. Therefore, as a small-business owner, you are in the trenches, so to speak, fighting a global battle to save a planet that has been taken for granted by some and exploited by other businesses for way too long.

As time moves forward the hope is that the 22 green businesses highlighted in Chapter 2, and the many new ones that will emerge in the coming years, can make sustainability a "business basic" rather than an alternative to the status quo. The hope is that the next generation will not have to think about opening a "green" business, but will do so by the mere example of how to start a business, any business. It all comes down to the mindset in which entrepreneurs approach their new opportunities.

There will always be the hard-edged salesperson who won't think twice about selling toxic products in nonrecyclable packaging made by child laborers if it will make a profit. There is still a segment of the business world made up of the cold and calculating sales mentality that worships the mighty dollar at any and all cost. These individuals won't be entertaining notions of saving the environment very soon. The hope is that as the future generation of today's environmentally and socially conscious business owners mature, that these become the exceptions and in time the dinosaurs of the business world.

And finally, yes, the idea of a business is to make a profit. Your greenest hopes and dreams are squashed if your business folds, so you may need to cut corners financially, and make sacrifices environmentally in the early going. You will hopefully reach a balance whereby financial and environmental success goes hand in hand, as Patagonia, Seventh Generation, and Pangea Organics can attest to. Your job, once you begin seeing profits, is to maintain that balance. Remember, there's a very fine line between green and greed.

# Appendix
## Green Business Resources

This appendix is designed to launch your developing green business. Although the list is extensive, it is by no means complete. It is one of the wonders of the internet age that at your fingertips, 24/7, you have the virtual world at the ready.

Choose your favorite search engine and start surfing. This is especially important when researching local or regional vendors and associations. Most of the sources listed here are national. You'll want to let your own fingers do the virtual walking when it comes time to finding local sources.

## Green Resource Websites

20/20 Vision.org, 2020vision.org

Air & Waste Management Association, awma.org

Alliance for America, allianceforamerica.org

Alliance to Save Energy, ase.org

American Council for an Energy Efficient Economy, aceee.org

American Forest & Paper Association, afandpa.org

American Wind Energy Association, awea.org

*Bio-plastics* magazine, bioplasticsmagazine.com

Better World Club, betterworldclub.com

Business & Institutional Furniture Manufacturer's Association, bifma.org

Carbon Fund, carbonfund.org

Care2 Network, care2.com

Center for Biological Diversity, biologicaldiversity.org

Center for Small Business & the Environment, geocities.com/aboutcsbe

CleanAir-CoolPlanet, cleanair-coolplanet.org

Computer Recycling, computerrecyclingdirectory.com

Conservation International, conservation.org

Conservatree, conservatree.com

Container Recycling Institute, container-recycling.org

Corporate Social Responsibility Newswire, csrwire.com.

Earthwatch, earthwatch.org

Eco Businesslinks Environmental Directory, ecobusinesslinks.com

Eco-Cell, eco-cell.org/locate_recycler.asp.

Eco-Office, eco-office.com

EcoMall, ecomall.com

Energy Savers, energysavers.gov

Energy Star, energystar.com

Envirolink Network, envirolink.org

Environmental Protection Agency (EPA), epa.gov

Environmental Technology Council, etc.org

Fair Trade Certified, transfairusa.org

Fair Trade Federation (FTF), fairtradefederation.org

Fairtrade Labeling Organization International, fairtrade.net

Forest Stewardship Council, fsc.org

Green Biz Leaders, greenbizleaders.com

Green Building Exchange, greenbuildingexchange.com

Green Business Alliance, greenbusinessalliance.com

Green Globe, ec3global.com

Green Pages Co-op, greenpages.org

Green Seal, greenseal.org

GreenBiz, greenbiz.com

GreenBlue, greenblue.org

Greenguard, greenguard.org

Interfaith Center on Corporate Responsibility, iccr.org

National Brownfield Association, brownfieldassociation.org

National Recycling Coalition, nrc-recycle.org

One Percent for the Planet, onepercentfortheplanet.org

Planet Green, planetgreen.com

Recellular, recellular.com/recycling

RideSpring, ridespring.com

Social Funds, socialfunds.com.

Social Investment Forum, socialinvest.org

The Daily Green, thedailygreen.com

Treehugger, treehugger.com

United States Department of Energy, Office of Energy Efficiency and Renewable Energy, eere.energy.gov

United States Green Building Council (USGBC—developers of the LEED ratings system), usgbc.org

ZeroFootprint.com, zerofootprint.com

Zipcar, zipcar.com

## Our 22 Green Business Examples

Chokola'j, chokolajchocolate.com

▲

Clif Bar & Company, clifbar.com

Electric Body, electricbody.com

Green Key Real Estate (and The Evergreen Group), greenkeyrealestate.com

Green Mountain Coffee Roasters, greenmountaincoffee.com

GreeNow, greenow.org

Inu Treats, inutreats.com

ITySE, ityse.biz

Kettle Foods, kettlefoods.com

Montana Stones, montanastones.com

New Belgium Brewery, newbelgium.com

Newman's Own Organics, newmansownorganics.com

New Tech Recycling, newtechrecycling.com

Odorzout, odorzout.com or 88stink.com

Pangea Organics, pangeaorganics.com

Patagonia, patagonia.com

Pizza Fusion, pizzafusion.com

Selfish Box, selfishbox.com

Seventh Generation, seventhgeneration.com

Solar Wind Works, solarwindworks.com

Sum-Bo-Shine, sumboshine.com

WeWe Clothing, weweclothing.com

Wild Dill, wilddill.com

# Business Resources
## United States Government Agencies and Business Associations

*United States Small Business Administration (SBA)*
409 Third Street SW
Washington, DC 20416
(800) 827-5722
sba.org

The U.S. Small Business Administration provides new entrepreneurs and existing business owners with financial, technical, and management resources to start, operate, and grow a business. To find your local SBA office, log on to sba.org/regions/states.html.

SBA Services and Products for Entrepreneurs

U.S. SBA Small Business Start-Up Kit, sba. gov/starting/indexstartup.html.

U.S. SBA Business Training Seminars and Courses, sba.gov/starting/indextraining.html.

U.S. SBA Business Plan: Road Map to Success, sba.gov/indexbusplans.html.

U.S. SBA Business Financing and Loan Program, sba.gov/financing

United States Patent and Trademark Office

*Internal Revenue Service (IRS)*
United States Department of the Treasury
1111 Constitution Avenue NW
Washington, DC 20224
(202) 622-5164
irs.ustreas.gov

*Service Corps of Retired Executives (SCORE)*
409 Third Street SW, 6th Floor
Washington, DC 20024
(800) 634-0245
score.org

*U.S. Department of Labor*
200 Constitution Avenue NW Room S-1032
Washington, DC 20210
(866) 4-USA-DOL
dol.gov

*U.S. Chamber of Commerce*
1615 H Street NW
Washington, DC 20062-2000
(202) 659-6000
uschamber.com

# Business Websites, including Business Magazines, Newspapers, and Professional Organizations and Associations

*Advertising Age* and *American Demographics*, adage.com

American Home Business Association, homebusiness.com

American Institute of Architects, aia.org

Biz Tradeshows, biztradeshows.com

*Black Enterprise* magazine, blackenterprise.com

*Business 2.0* magazine, business2.0.com

Business Know-How, businessknowhow.com

Business Network International, bni.com

*Business Week*, businessweek.com

*Canadian Business* magazine, canadianbusiness.com

*Entrepreneur* magazine, entrepreneur.com/magazine

Entrepreneur Online, entrepreneur.com

*Family Business* magazine, familybusinessmagazine.com

*Forbes*, forbes.com

*Inc.* magazine, inc.com

International Franchise Association (IFA), franchise.org

Market Research, marketresearch.com

National Venture Capital Association, nvca.org

Network Solutions, networksolutions.com

News Link, newslink.org

PC Magazine, *pcmag.com*

Smart Biz, smartbiz.com

Small Business Loans Online, smallbusinessloans.com

*Small Business Opportunities*, sbomag.com

Trade Show Exhibitors Association, tsea.org

V Finance, vfinance.com

*Wall Street Journal*, wsj.com

*Washington Business Journal*, washington.bizjournals.com/washington

# Office Supplies

Business Supply, business-supply.com

Discounted Office Supply, discountedofficesupply.com

Green Earth Office Supply, http://greenearthofficesupply.stores.yahoo.net

Green Light Office Supplies, greenlightoffice.com

Green Office Supplies, greenofficesupplies.com

Office Depot, officedepot.com

Office Max, officemax.com

Staples, staples.com

The Green Office, thegreenoffice.com

# Glossary

**Benchmarks.** A benchmark is a point of reference by which something can be measured, such as your carbon footprint, sustainability, and/or your business profitability. As a business owner, you can set up benchmarks that you would like to reach at a pre-determined time and then measure your success against those markers.

**Biodegradable.** The ability of a substance to be broken down physically and/or chemically by microorganisms. Natural and organic products are typically biodegradable while many synthetic plastics or materials like polyester generally are not.

**Biodiesel.** A renewable type of diesel fuel derived from various organic feedstock including vegetable oils and animal fats, for use in compression ignition. Biodiesel is cleaner and more energy efficient (limits $CO_2$ emissions) than petroleum-based fuels.

**Business plan.** A comprehensive document clearly outlining the future of a business including all areas of operations, marketing, and management. A business plan is used to generate funding and for the business owner to measure the ongoing progress of the business.

**Business structure.** Typically refers to the organizational framework in which the business will operate. Most common are sole proprietorship, corporation, or limited liability corporation.

**Carbon footprint.** A measure of the amount of carbon dioxide or $CO_2$ emitted by a business as part of its daily operations.

**Carbon neutral.** Also known as carbon zero, this is where you are either emitting no $CO_2$ into the atmosphere or balancing the amount of $CO_2$ emitted in other another manner.

**Carbon offsets.** A means of achieving carbon neutrality by paying for ecological and environmentally beneficial projects in other parts of the country or the world to balance the amount of $CO_2$ your business is emitting into the atmosphere. (Green Tags for travel are a similar concept.)

**Competitive edge.** Your advantage over your competition.

**Composting.** A process of utilizing organic materials (typically garbage and scraps) to create a fertilizer for soil and plants.

**Credit rating.** A numerical score used by banks and lenders to evaluate the likelihood of a borrower defaulting on a loan.

**Demographics.** Researched information about the lifestyles, habits, spending, age, social grade, income, and other characteristics of specific populations.

**Eco-friendly (also environmentally friendly).** Ways and means of operating a business or using materials and products that are not harmful to the planet by way of greenhouse gas, $CO_2$ emissions, being non-biodegradable, or being toxic.

**Energy star.** A joint program of the U.S. Environmental Protection Agency and the U.S. Department of Energy that provides designation of products identified as energy-efficient.

**Fair trade.** Making sure that products imported and exported internationally are produced under fair conditions and sold or purchased under reasonable agreements for both sides.

**Global warming.** The warming of the earth's atmosphere because greenhouses gasses are preventing the heat from escaping (see *greenhouse effect*).

**Green building.** The practice of building structures utilizing environmentally friendly materials and designed to operate in an ecological manner that uses natural resources and leaves a minimal carbon footprint.

**Greenhouse effect.** The earth's heat being held in place by gasses in the earth's atmosphere such as carbon dioxide ($CO_2$), methane ($CH_4$), and nitrous oxide ($N_2O$) (called greenhouses gasses). The result is *global warming*. This is similar to the manner in which a greenhouse maintains heat.

**Greenwashing.** The practice of misleading the public by creating a pro-environmental image while not actually following environmental and/or ecological practices.

**Hybrid car.** An automobile that uses both a combustible (fossil-fuel-burning) engine and an electric motor powered by batteries.

**Indoor air quality.** The quality of the air within your workplace. Your goal is non-toxicity or *Volatile Organic Compounds* (see below).

**Landfill.** A means of final disposal of solid waste on land. The refuse/waste is compacted and spread out in layers of soil, remaining there for years.

**LEED-certified.** A designation by the U.S. Green Building Council's Leadership in Energy and Environmental Design (LEED) indicating that either a building, architect, or the material used in the building process meets sustainable green building and development standards.

**Lifecycle.** The course of a product from the growth of initial materials to the final end of the product's components either being recycled or ending up as waste.

**Media kit.** A public relations package sent to the media or clients you are wishing to impress that is usually displayed in a pocket folder. Typically you include recent press releases, articles featuring your business, relevant photos, and background on your company.

**Organic.** Naturally grown materials without the use of fossil fuels or any types of chemicals.

**Recycling.** The broad term used to indicate that the materials used in a product will be part of a process that allows them to be reused in another product. There are numerous manners in which various materials, such as plastics, are melted down in the recycling process. Recycling is also often used to refer to the reuse of a product by one person after it has been used by another, thus maintaining the usefulness of the item.

**Renewable energy.** Energy from resources that can keep producing indefinitely without being depleted, such as solar and wind power.

**Reuse.** Utilizing a product for another purpose rather than its initial intended purpose to maintain the life and usefulness of the product. Unlike recycling, the item is typically not altered or does not change shape.

**Socially responsible.** A manner of describing a business or organization that is proactive in terms of doing positive things for their employees and for their community and society at large.

**Socially responsible investing (SRI).** Investing in businesses, mutual funds, or other investment vehicles that use social and environmental criteria that mirror your own beliefs.

**Sustainability.** The practice of maintaining a lifecycle that goes from nature back to nature utilizing as minimal amount of manmade energy as possible.

**Target market.** A clearly defined segment of the overall population to which a business can market and promote its products and services for the intent of generating sales.

**Transparency.** The manner in which your goals, motives, and means of operations are clear and open to being observed or reviewed by the public at large.

**Volatile organic compounds (VOC).** Organic compounds that evaporate readily into the air. These are typically not good for air quality and include substances such as benzene, methylene chloride, and methyl chloroform.

**Waste management.** The process of finding and utilizing ways of limiting waste and/or reducing waste from ending up in landfill.

# Index

**A**

Advertising, 144–148
headlines, 148–149
*An Inconvenient Truth*, 9
Angel investors, 98
Appendix, green business resources, 179–185
Architect, finding a green, 63–64

**B**

Benchmarks, company, 174–175
Blogging, 144
Brochures, 145
Brokerage business, green, 3–4
Brownfields, 64–65
Builder, finding a green, 63–64
Building your green business, 51–68
from the ground up, 61–62
Business
decisions, 15–37
goals, 18–19, 174–175
worksheet, 20
growth, managing, 171–175
needs and sustainable practices, integrating, 4, 11–14
particulars of your, 60–61
plan, 90–96
resources, 179–185
structure, choosing your, 54, 56–57
Business name
choosing and registering your, 51–54, 55–56
domain name, 53–54
worksheet, 55–56
Buzzword, "green" as new, 1–2

**C**

Carbon
footprint, calculating your, 2
neutrality, 12
offsets, 12–14
Chairs, office, 78
Charitable giving/alliances, 159–160
Chokola'j, chokolajchocolate.com, 33–34
Choosing the right business, 22–26
Clif Bar Company, clifbar.com, 27–28
Community, your, 122–124
Commuting, greener, 112–113

Competition, scouting the, 47–49
Competitive edge, finding a green, 8
Composting, 97
Computer considerations, 70–73
printers, friendly ways of using, 73–74
Contractor, finding a green, 63–64
Cost savings through rebates and government support for building green or using renewable energy, 12
Customers
and market research, 39–50
"80-20 Rule," 49
what do they want?, 40–42

**D**
Doing for others, 159–160
Domain name, 53–54

**E**
Eco-friendly
materials as marketing advantage, 8
policies, establishing them from the beginning, 9–10
Eco-lifecycle of a product, 6–7
Educating yourself through researching green business practices and green companies, 9
Education, green, 163–164
Electric Body, electricbody.com, 35
Employees
building a collective (team) mindset, 121–122
creating a socially responsible culture, 158–159
establishing a green business culture, 115–119
hiring like-minded, 8
protocol, green, 120–121
your green team, 115–122
Employment law, 7
Energy options, 65–66
Environmental
activities, hands-on involvement in, 9
causes, contributing profits to, 12
goals, 20–21
goals worksheet, 21
Environmental Protection Agency, help and financing programs, 99

Environmentally-oriented internet sites for exploring green business practices, 8, 9
Equipment, business, 69–85
startup costs, 70
Evergreen Group LLC, 30

**F**
Factory, green, 10
Fair trade practices/certified products, 160–161
Faking environmental concern, "greenwashers," 176
Farming and agricultural businesses, 25
Financial goals, 18
worksheet, 19
Financing, 87–100
Fliers, 145
Focus groups, 44–45
Friends and family financing, 97–98
Furniture, green office, 76–79
Future of green, 175–177

**G**
Global industrialization, not adding to problems caused by, 5
Glossary, 187–190
Goals, personal
defining your, 16–17
worksheet, 17
Gore, Al, 9, 176
Government agencies and business associations, US, 182–183
Government financing, 98–99
Green businesses, a look at twenty-two successful, 26–37, 181–182
Green Key Real Estate, greenkeyrealestate.com, 30
Green mindset, 7–9
Green Mountain Coffee Roasters, greenmountaincoffee.com, 28
GreenNow, greenow.org, 33
Growing it yourself, 108–109
Growth, managing business, 171–175

**H**
Habits, maintaining positive green, 172
Hiring like-minded people for your startup, 8

Homebased business, 11, 124–126
    growth of, 63
How to choose the right business for you,
    22–26

I

Incorporating, 54, 56
Industries that have not yet embraced green
    fully, business opportunities in, 8
Industry news, staying current with, 173–174
Internet
    advertising, 146
    presence, 80–81, 141–142
    sites for exploring green business practices,
        8, 9
Inu Treats, inutreats.com, 32
Inventory, 105– 106
Investing, socially responsible, 165–169
Investors, 87–100
    Angel, 98
iTySE, ityse.biz, 36

K

Kettle foods, kettlefoods.com, 28–29

L

Leasing *versus* buying and building, 62– 63
Lighting, office, 78–79
Limited liability corporation, LLC, 56–57
Loans. *See* Financing
Location, finding a green, 58–59, 64–65
Looking forward and looking back, 2–3

M

Magazine advertising, 145–146
Making money, 102–103
Manufacturing
    business, 24–24
    model, greener, 10
Market research, 39–50
    common errors, 50
    focus groups, 44–45
    niche markets, 46–47
    scouting the competition, 47–49
    target market, 42–44
    utilizing your, 45–46
    what do customers want?, 40–42

Marketing
    failures, 130
    green, 130–131
    plan, 128, 132
    promotion and advertising, 127–155
    success stories, 128–130
Membership in green organizations and associ-
    ations, 9
Milk, eco-lifecycle of, 6–7
Money, making, 102–103
Montana stones, montanastones.com, 35

N

Naming your business, 51–54
    worksheet, 55–56
New Belgium Brewery, newbelgium.com, 27
Newman's Own Organics, newmansownorganics
    .com, 31–
Newsletters, online, 142–144
Newspaper advertising, 145–146
Niche markets, 46–47

O

Odorzout, odorzout.com, 88stink.com, 32
Office
    equipment and furniture, 69–85
    green, 9–10
    suppliers, 185
    supplies, greener, 75–76
Online
    advertising, 146
    presence, 80–81, 141–142
    research, 8, 9
Operating costs, 84–85

P

Packaging and packing, sustainable, 109–110
Pangea Organics, pangeaorganics.com, 26–27
Paper
    minimizing use of, 76
    recycled, 4
Paper or plastic or neither, 10, 36
Partnerships, 57
Patagonia, patagonia.com, 27
Phillip Merrill Environmental Center, world's
    greenest building, 58
Pizza Fusion, pizzafusion.com, 29–30

Post World War II era industrial expansion and lack of environmental management, 4
Press releases, 137–141
    sample #1, 150–152
    sample #2, 153–155
Pricing, 103–105
Printing, green, 79
Products, manufacturing environmentally-friendly, 107–109
Promotion, 133–135
Public relations, 135–141
    defining your objectives, 136

**R**

Radio advertising, 146–147
Recognition, company, 172–173
Reducing, reusing, recycling, defined, 5
Retail business, launching a green, 10

**S**

Sampson, Karel J., 25
SCORE (Service Corps of Retired Executives), mentoring help from, 95
Self-financing, 100
Selfish Box, selfishbox.com, 34
Service oriented business, 23–24, 111–112
Seventh Generation, seventhgeneration.com, 29
Shipping
    and transportation needs, 60
    greener, 111
Small Business Administration (SBA), loans and help from, 95, 98–99
Social responsibility, 7, 157–169
Solar panels, 66–67
Solar Wind Works, solarwindworks.com, 30–31
Sole proprietorship, 54
Spending more now to save more later, 12
Startup costs, 81–83
    worksheet, 82–83
Store, green, 10

Successful green businesses, a look at twenty-two, 26–37, 181–182
Sum-Bo-Shine, shumboshine.com, 34–35
Suppliers, green, 106–107
Sustainability
    as underpinning of green business, 2
    formal definition of, 4
    plan, 96–97
    sustaining, 171–177
    understanding, 3–5

**T**

Target market, exploring your, 42–44
Teaming up with like-minded companies, 113
Telephone systems, 74
Television advertising, 147–148
*The 4 E's: Entrepreneurship, Economy, Ecology, and the Ego!* by Karel J. Sampson, PhD, 25

**V**

Venture capital, 99–100

**W**

Website
    company, 141–142
    designer, 80–81
Websites
    business magazines, newspapers, professional organizations and associations, 184–185
    for green resources, 179–180
WeWe Clothing, weweclothing.com, 31
Wild Dill, wilddill.com, 36–37
Wind turbines, 66–67
Work environment, green, 161–163
World's greenest building, 58

**Z**

Zoning regulations, 57